D0500474

Where You Go

Where You Go

Life Lessons from My Father

Charlotte Pence

CENTER
STREET

New York Nashville

Center Street
Hachette Book Group
1290 Avenue of the Americas
New York, NY 10104

www.CenterStreet.com

Printed in the United States of America

First Edition: October 2018

Center Street is a division of Hachette Book Group, Inc.
The Center Street name and logo are trademarks of Hachette Book Group, Inc.

The publisher is not responsible for websites (or their content) that are not owned by the publisher.

The Hachette Speakers Bureau provides a wide range of authors for speaking events. To find out more, go to www.HachetteSpeakersBureau.com or call (866) 376-6591.

Unless otherwise noted, photos are courtesy of the author.

Scriptures are taken from The Holy Bible: New International Version®, NIV® Copyright © 1973, 1978, 1984, 2011 by Biblica, Inc.® Used by permission. All rights reserved worldwide.

Library of Congress Control Number: 2018952711

ISBNs: 978-1-5460-7618-6 (hardcover), 978-1-5460-7615-5 (ebook)

Printed in the United States of America

LSC-C

10 9 8 7 6 5 4 3 2 1

This book is for my very first readers and listeners—
my beloved family:
Dad
Mom
Michael and Sarah
Audrey

Contents

Foreword

Vice President Mike Pence

Charlotte Rose Pence came into this world on Friday, June 25, 1993, and she has been a wonder and a blessing in our lives ever since.

Karen and I couldn't be more proud of all our kids—a son who is a United States Marine with a strong and talented wife, and another daughter who is studying law at one of the nation's premier schools and who has a heart for the wider world. But Charlotte was the only one of our children whose path we saw from early on: Charlotte Pence is a writer.

As a little girl sandwiched between a precocious older brother and a sweet baby sister, Charlotte was the classic middle child—quiet, helpful, nurturing, and always watching everything that was happening around her. You could see it in her eyes, while even at a very young age, she would be standing off to the side as our family went through the hustle and bustle of public life.

She didn't say much, but she was always observing, learning, and—as this book attests—she was always storing up precious memories in that tender heart. Now we know it was all so she could tell better stories later.

Charlotte has always been a storyteller. She and her sister shared a small bedroom for most of their childhood and it didn't take us long to realize that the murmuring we heard behind closed doors after bedtime prayers was Charlotte telling Audrey a story—made up as she went along—just to help her little sister fall asleep.

One of my most vivid images of her youth was minted one day when I looked out the kitchen window of our house only to see Charlotte sitting in the grass facing an assembled audience of all her stuffed animals and dolls. Charlotte was telling them a story.

As my political career was just getting started and our prospects for public service were widening before us, knowing her love of writing, I would occasionally tease her that someday she would "write a book about her old Dad," never really thinking she would. Whenever I said it, Charlotte would roll her eyes and say, "sure Dad" but give me that soft smile of encouragement that told me she thought that someday she might just do that.

And now, here we are—not so many years from all those precious memories—and our remarkable daughter has done just that with the publication of *Where You Go*. As you read this book, I am confident you will come to appreciate her unique ability to communicate with the written word.

In the pages of this book, just like the essays she published during her time studying at the University of Oxford and the Instagram account for her pet rabbit that would attract 30,000 followers and inspire her first book, *Marlon Bundo's A Day in the Life of the Vice President* (Regnery, 2018), you will see that Charlotte Pence just has a way of writing that elevates while still speaking in the voice of her generation.

You will see what her mother and I have seen for many years—a gifted pen, an authentic voice, and a capacity to tell stories that convey timeless truth with humility and humor. You will also see that this book is not so much about her "old Dad," but it is about our family. Our Charlotte has preserved moments from our little family's story that I cannot read without tears from a heart grateful for God's grace. I suspect our story is not so different from yours, and my hope is that the lessons she so tenderly conveys here will resonate and encourage you and many American families who have faced choices, challenges, and triumphs, only to learn that those whom you love and the faith you share are what matter most. Charlotte has captured that truth in this winsome book and my prayer is that it will be as much a blessing to you as our writer has been to us every day of her life.

Signed,
Mike Pence
Proud Father and Vice President of the United States
May 2018
Washington, D.C.

I shall be telling this with a sigh
Somewhere ages and ages hence:
Two roads diverged in a wood, and I—I took the one less traveled by,
And that has made all the difference.

—Robert Frost, "The Road Not Taken"

Preface

Dear Reader,

I was always certain I would write this book.

I was not certain anyone would read it other than my family.

This book has evolved from the inclination I first had when I was seven years old to write about my father. Back then, in a small notebook, I wrote Dad's biography, scribbling words about his childhood and career—how he had grown up one of six kids, fulfilled his dream of becoming a lawyer, and became a talk radio host, and later a congressman. In the book, I included tiny drawings of our family (and there was probably a Capitol dome among the illustrations). I was excited to give Dad this gift: I believed that he saw me as a storyteller, even from the time I was a child. Dad indeed cherished my gift, and he always encouraged me to pursue my dream. "You're a writer," he said. Often, during special times with family, Dad would wink at me and say, "You'll put this in a book one day, Booh" (his nickname for me since I was little).

When I was in middle school, I gave Dad a homemade gift for Father's Day—another book, whose cover read, *The Lessons You Have Taught Me*. It was tiny and nondescript, and I had scribbled on each page a different sentence or phrase to name a lesson that Dad had either spoken or shown to me throughout my childhood. To this day, he keeps it in the top drawer of his desk and I hope he sometimes pulls it out and flips through it, perhaps on days when he needs a reminder there are people who are watching him, who see him, and who love him.

The lessons inside that little book are as follows:

1. *Lead by example.*
2. *An animated movie is always a good idea.*
3. *Ride horses every chance you get.*
4. *Never shout. Anger does not inspire.*
5. *Three things: Devotions, Studies, and Exercise.*
6. *Call cashiers by the name on their name tag. See everyone.*
7. *Read.*
8. *Write.*
9. *The safest place to be is in the center of God's will.*
10. *When you miss your chance to climb that Irish hill again, go back.*
11. *Love one person deeply and truly.*
12. *Be honest in all things—especially the small things.*
13. *Never end a good conversation short.*
14. *Check on people.*
15. *Learn from history. Know your idols.*
16. *Believe in your dreams. A cornfield to the Capitol.*
17. *If you lose your family, nothing else will matter much.*
18. *Never be too busy for yardwork and a nap on Sundays.*
19. *Take long drives.*
20. *Never let anyone tell you that you can't.*

That was where it ended the first time around, but over the years I made some additions:

21. *Be fascinated by things. Never let the invention of an airplane be something that you are not impressed with.*

22. *Know where you come from.*
23. *At an airport, always go to the gate first.*
24. *Never stop believing in magic.*

I often say I am more comfortable behind the camera than in front of it. This is true of writing as well, and I have spent my life observing those around me and oftentimes writing it down. This is especially true when it comes to lessons I have learned from my family members, and my dad, in particular. His words of wisdom remain in my memory, but over the years, I have felt the need to write them down too. Those observations, thoughts, and pieces of advice eventually found their way into this book I write now.

I hope to shed some light on who Dad is as a father, a leader, and a person. I hope also to share some of the inside stories of our family, so that you, too, can learn from them. Dad often says that he is "a Christian, a conservative, and a Republican—in that order." It is my desire to detail just what that means in our family— not only through his political role, but also in our day-to-day life. As I have continued to develop this craft of writing from a young age, the story of our life has only gotten more exciting. The plot has resulted in much more than I could have imagined, and the example he and Mom have been for me throughout all the twists and turns has been essential in shaping the person I am today. I hope to shed light on who my parents are, what they have been for me, and the lessons Dad has taught me. He not only inspires me through his role as a public figure, but also, more importantly, through my interactions with him as a daughter who could not have asked for a better dad.

In college, my parents were the kind who actually encouraged me to pursue subjects I was interested in, even ones that could have made other moms and dads nervous. I double-majored in creative writing and screenwriting. When I considered studying abroad, Dad suggested Oxford, "because C. S. Lewis went there." I remember laughing, insisting, "I can't get in *there*, Dad," but I applied and was ecstatic to be accepted and to spend a year living in that wonderful ancient city. When my parents encouraged me to believe in myself, it made my dreams seem attainable. I had the experience of a lifetime where I studied alongside the talented students I met and was challenged by the great professors of Oxford. I also spread my writing wings and wrote for local publications and enjoyed working in the St. Catherine's dining hall in the evenings.

My parents encouraged me to go after my dreams, and they taught me to focus my passions to make a positive difference in the world, just as I had grown up watching them do. In college, my love of stories led me into documentary filmmaking, where I was most inspired while chronicling the lives of people who were dedicated to helping others. They helped me understand how even our smallest actions can be truly powerful. Motivated by this example, and using my own voice, I hope to uplift those who need it by sharing the pieces of wisdom from the man, and the woman, whom I admire most.

This book of "lessons from my father" is not complete—and not even possible—without lessons from my mom, too. Any memory of Dad and me inevitably includes Mom. She is forever there, right beside him, and she is the necessary and subconscious steadiness that keeps our family close no matter what. My parents are a team, two people who act as one, and there is no lesson I have learned from my dad that is not from my mom as well. They better each other with their differences and make one another stronger in their similarities. Mom is the ever-present guiding force, the ultimate protector, and the shining light when the path is uncertain. And the lessons I have learned from my father are completed by her constant presence, her unwavering support, and her faithful, candid spirit. I hope to be like her, to emulate her courage, strength, and compassion in every choice I make. Both of my parents continue to teach me the lessons of this book every day with the lives they lead and through the words they pass on.

Through writing this book, I attempt to pay tribute to the impact both my dad and mom have had on my life, but I won't stop there. I will try to thank and honor them through the life I choose to lead and by passing their wisdom down to my own children one day.

The stories you will find here are primarily from the life-changing months of July 2016 to August 2017. However, some accounts extend back into the parts of my memory reserved for childhood experiences, and some reach closer to the present, to what has taken place since my father became vice president of the United States.

As fate determined, some of the most pivotal events of my family's life fell directly after I graduated from college. My father was nominated to be Donald Trump's vice presidential running mate; he accepted the nomination and assumed his place on the campaign trail. As a result, summer '16 to '17 turned into a gap year for me, a year off in between college and officially entering the full-time workforce. I lived at home, working remotely part-time, and joined my parents as they campaigned across America. We all adjusted to the new adventure together.

It was all unplanned, the path unknown, and I wouldn't go back and change it for anything. For a lover of stories, my family, and my country, it was the ultimate experience.

While on the campaign trail, *Glamour* magazine reached out

to me to write a story about my travels across America with my parents. I wrote about Dad and the lessons he taught me on that journey and throughout my entire life. Published in October 2016, the article was called "Mike Pence's Daughter Reveals the Lessons Her Father Taught Her." In a way, that article ultimately led me to write this book.

Like an expansion of my childhood tribute to Dad, *The Lessons You Have Taught Me*, I drafted this book over the last year, composed from memories, my journal writings, scrap paper notes, thoughts, and stories told to friends and later transferred to the page. I have been writing it much longer than that, though. It has been waiting to be written for decades, even before I was born.

These accounts are about my family and our life, the ordinary and extraordinary experiences we've shared, and what we've taken from them. I hope you will apply our memories to your own and see the comparisons where they lie. I believe we are not all that different from one another, and I hope these stories will encourage you, as they have me. They have inspired me throughout my life. They are the jumping-off point from wherever I start. They are the places I land when I need to be reminded of the magic in the world and of the love we have for one another no matter what. Every life lesson from my dad, every moment we shared on his journey to the White House, every memory from my childhood, every conversation I've had with my brother and his wife, every adventure taken with my sister and piece of advice received from my mom can be found in the fabric of these pages. I hope the same influences will also be evident in every other part of my life and work.

These stories made me who I am. They led my family to the journey that began in 2016, to the new chapter we're now writing within our lives, in the day-to-day decisions and moments we share, and they will continue to lead us beyond.

I have faith in these stories. I have faith in God that He will lead us where He wants us to go, and my family will embrace the adventures He takes us on even when the road seems uncertain.

This collection is for us, but it is for you, too.

Come along with me, and I will show you.

But first there is something you should know about us.

Where You Go

Chapter One

Where You Go

But Ruth replied, "Don't urge me to leave you or to turn back from
  you.
Where you go I will go, and where you stay I will stay.
Your people will be my people and your God my God."

—Ruth 1:16

This verse, commonly quoted in the Pence family, holds the
truth of how we navigate life and all it brings. It is our beacon. It has defined our vision, led us forward, and kept us
from turning too frequently sideways or backward in the midst of
struggle. It comes from the Book of Ruth in the Old Testament. In
this story, Ruth is a young woman whose husband dies shortly after
they wed. Naomi, Ruth's mother-in-law, tells Ruth to leave, to have
her own life, and not to come and live with her anymore, but Ruth
won't leave the elderly woman behind. What would have become
of her? Ruth tells her that they are family, they are one unit now,
and therefore wherever life takes Naomi, Ruth will follow.

The implications of this action were so grand because Ruth
essentially saved Naomi's life by staying with her and promising
to provide for her in her old age, but that also meant Ruth had to

leave her own culture and people forever. Ruth pledged to provide Naomi with a new family and a means of prosperity while leaving comfort behind. Staying with Naomi, she would be in a place where she was considered an outsider, an immigrant in a foreign land.

Tim Keller gives a sermon on this passage, in which he says, "[Ruth] suddenly realized, 'If I obey God I may not have the life I expected, but I will have a better one. If I give up my definition of "good," God will give me back—maybe not the "good life" I wanted—but the great life.'"* In this ancient story, told in hindsight and passed down for generations, Ruth's choice may appear easy because we know everything works out well for her. The truth is, we never know in the individual moments how our decisions will impact the future. We cannot be sure that if we follow what we believe to be God's calling and plan for our life, things will be fine. In fact, we know the opposite is true, which makes these decisions all the more difficult. No matter your religious affiliation, I believe Ruth's courage can be admired and emulated in all walks of life.

Like Ruth's story, this book is also written in hindsight. It is a culmination of the months and years of *after*, with observations of *during*, and lessons from *before*. It attempts to provide a firsthand account from someone who witnessed the 2016 presidential campaign from the trail and how it impacted the Pences as a family—as *my* family. From an outside perspective, another vantage point than ours, it may seem as though everything fell together seamlessly or our movements were perfectly placed, as is the inevitable result of my retelling what we've already lived. But I would ask you,

---

* "An Immigrant's Courage," Timothy Keller Sermons Podcast by Gospel in Life, accessed March 2018. https://www.acast.com/timothykellersermonspodcastby gospelinlife/an-immigrants-courage

the reader, to remember this: The end result of anything is simply a combination of small decisions made along the way that are often overlooked or forgotten. The times in our lives when we can either remain where we're comfortable or step out in faith toward the unknown, while difficult, can often be the most powerful and rewarding.

These stories share what happened to my family, who when faced with monumental decisions, went forth in faith and little else.

When thinking about a title for this book, I had a few in mind. They were all winks to my family members, inside nudges that I hoped would translate as a warm embrace in their hearts when they read them. But as I continued to think about what needed to be said about my family in this book, what creates the foundation for the stories I share with you and other readers, it was Ruth's promise to Naomi.

It was essentially what we told one another when Dad became a candidate for vice president of the United States.

It was literally what I told my parents when it was finalized they would be traveling for several months on the campaign trail.

It was what I said, again, when we won the election and were transplanted back to Washington, D.C., where we had lived while Dad served in Congress.

It is what Mom says to Dad with every knowing glance.

It is what he says back when he reaches out his hand.

It is what we say despite the arguments, the disagreements, the debates, and the struggles we have, along with every other family in the world.

It is what we do.

Where you go, I will go, too.

Chapter Two

No Flapping

Like a seed in the snow
I've been buried to grow
For your promise is loyal
From seed to sequoia
—Hillsong Worship, "Seasons"

I wouldn't have minded growing up in one house, on one street, with one yard we would adjust, improve, plan, and landscape all our lives. My parents envisioned this, too. They planned to live it. In the backyard of the little house they built in Indianapolis, Indiana, Mom planted a dogwood tree for each of her children when we were born, perhaps envisioning her grandchildren playing beneath them. But that was not to be. The trees are full grown now, and I hope some big or little kid found shade beneath them at one point in his or her life, or jumped in their leaves on a crisp, Indiana fall day.

Thinking back on my childhood, times of transition are often marked with moving, with leaving homes, and with traveling someplace unfamiliar and discovering uncharted territory.

When Dad was elected as an Indiana congressman in 2000, we followed him to live in Washington, D.C. My parents sold the house they had built in Indianapolis, and we headed east to start anew with no family or friends to go with us. Many congressional families decide to stay in their home states instead, but we didn't want Dad to travel back and forth so much. The best thing about growing up was not that Dad was in Congress. It was that he was home for dinner almost every night. We got to see him; we knew him.

Although my parents sold the first Indianapolis house when we moved to Washington, D.C., there was another little place we got to call home in southern Indiana, in Columbus. There we kept a one-story ranch house surrounded by miles and miles of farmland as far as the eye could see. This was the Indiana house we called home, heading back to it for holidays, summers, campaign events, and family reunions. Even though my parents had to leave the house they had imagined raising their children in, God provided another home where we would make our memories. The truth is, the importance was never found in the houses or the cities in which we lived. It never has been or will be. We found our value and strength in one another and time spent together.

When Dad ran for governor of Indiana in 2012, however, we finally let go of the Columbus, Indiana, home, too. We sold it and followed him to Indianapolis once again, where we rented a home during the election. As always, it was important for us all to be together. He and Mom said a final goodbye to the Columbus house we had been raised in, remembering the little Indiana home and D.C., too. Dad held Mom's hand as they drove away, everything packed up and gone.

"Thanks for coming with me," he said. "Thank you for not letting me miss this."

What he meant by "this," was "us." He didn't miss watching his kids grow up. We were a part of his life as much as he was a part of ours—and that included his political life and all it would eventually become.

A few times growing up, we went back and saw the trees Mom had planted at that first house so many years ago. We looked up the hill we learned to ride bikes on, remembering it to have been a mountain peak of terror at the top and a roller coaster all the way down. Through adult eyes and in adulthood reality, it is just a slight incline on the street.

Each time we were near the Indianapolis home, my parents asked, "Should we go see Sun Mountain [their name for the neighborhood]?" And we did. It must have been hard for them—to see the place in the driveway where we had once left our handprints in wet cement and sketched the date underneath. Back before everything had begun—the run for Congress, the move, the move back, and the race for governor. They must have looked at each other with knowing smiles, being the only two with a clear memory of the little ones we were back then.

Now that I think back on it, I remember us only visiting the cement handprints one time. We stuck our hands in the indentations our toddler selves had made, our fingers spilling over the sides, and Dad took a few pictures before we went on our way. Whenever we drove past again, we didn't stop to put our hands in the prints to see how much we had grown. We looked at the house, we waved to the neighborhood, but if we stopped, we stayed away from the indentations. It was probably not intentional, but maybe subconsciously we knew we couldn't do it again. Simply seeing the house was enough to bring us all back, to remember what could have been if my parents had stayed there and Dad had continued his radio career instead of running for Congress. I know the high school I would have gone to, and I have a good idea of the friendships I would have developed, because I had already made some of those friends before we left.

And the handprints might just have been too much. To see how we had grown larger than them, outside of them, we would have had to acknowledge how much we had all changed, and splintered, and torn as we discovered ourselves in a new fated environment, that we were no longer the people we used to be—both physically and emotionally. My parents had taken a chance on Dad's dreams, and it had pushed us into the unknown. We had been challenged; we had grown up. To go back to the handprints more than once would have been to realize this change more fully and perhaps a little forlornly. Our physical bodies would have taken up more space than the impressions our former, younger selves had left behind to be remembered by. So, we offered a farewell to what our lives could have been and paid homage to the memories that would have taken place in that home, in that life.

We could have stopped there—and ended the sentiment with a sense of sadness, with memories and feelings of "what could have been." But to do that would be to miss the point—to miss the grand possibilities our lives can turn into if we chase our dreams, if we run into the open field of unknown futures and we trust in the faith that guides us forward. This was what my parents did, and I will be forever grateful to them for this.

Now all I can do is thank Karen Pence of 1994, who planted those saplings, and Mike of 1995, who got his three toddlers together in the backyard on a Saturday afternoon to giggle and squirm and feel the mush of the drying concrete beneath our fingers as we left a permanent wave into the future, a greeting and a goodbye. They showed me how to remember the sweet memories of the past, but also how to forge ahead fearlessly into the future, holding the hands of the ones you love.

While I honor the treasures of these early 1990s memories, I am even more thankful to Karen and Mike of 1999, who took a chance on another dream, who brought their children with them, who taught them they could be anyone they wanted to be and who didn't let material items and set plans determine the future direction of their lives. When thinking back on this time, Jonah 2:8, often quoted by Mom and Dad, comes to mind: "Those who cling to worthless idols forfeit the grace that could be theirs." My parents often quote this verse to me when material possessions, relationships, or worldly ambitions begin to seep into my consciousness and distract me from the ultimate truth: God has a plan for us that is greater than any we may have for ourselves. We need only to trust Him and follow where He leads.

The '90s versions of my parents, Mike and Karen, are the ones who made the stories. And ours are the stories I tell. These stories are the culmination of many small decisions along the way, yes, but this specific one started on a mountainside during a family vacation in 1999. If not for one moment, one conversation with Mom, our lives may have turned out quite differently and Dad may have never run for Congress at all.

———

There is a legend often told in our family. To understand this book, you must understand us, and to understand us, you must hear it. It is the reason, the calling card, the driving force, the backdrop, and the answers to the "whys" you will undoubtedly have. Every friend, confidant, family member, and staff member of the Pence family has been told this story at some point in their interaction with us. Now you are one of them; you are part of the family, and so you must hear it, too.

Dad often quotes Reagan, who said, "The outside of a horse is good for the inside of a man," and so growing up whenever we had the funds, the time, and Mom let him pick the spot, he always made a point to take us where there were horses, woods, and log cabins.

Family vacations are some of my favorite memories because I was (and still am) a kid with a big imagination. In the summer of 1999, my family vacationed on a ranch in Colorado. We hiked or rode horses on trails during the day, cozied up to campfires at night, and spent time exploring together. When we went to the ranch, not only was it exciting for me to be in a place that so resembled Narnia, but I was also able to come up with my own stories there—the world was whatever I wanted it to be, and time stood still once we entered the great outdoors. Perhaps I caught some feeling in the air on that particular trip, too. My subconscious tapped into the possibilities the future held for my family on those mountainsides and it never really let go.

As the legend goes, my parents were on a trail ride when they stopped to look out at the view together. Dad had been considering something big for their future and this trip was supposed to help both of them clear their minds to make a decision. Unbeknownst to us kids, this was when our lives changed—things were never going to be the same again.

The Mike Pence Show was a syndicated radio talk show in Indiana at the time, and it was really taking off. Dad called it "Rush Limbaugh on decaf," and so it was. He held interviews with esteemed individuals, politicians, and local authorities, and he discussed the present-day issues facing Indiana and the nation. It was good practice for where his career was headed—even though he didn't know it at the time. He loved it, too. He always had a special place in his heart for the media and still does. He had fun at that job. He was truly himself.

About ten years earlier, in 1988, and again in 1990, Dad had run for Congress and lost both times. It was crushing to him then, but it made him put his whole heart into starting his radio show. It was actually Mom's idea, as you will come to find all good things are, and at the time of our ranch vacation, it was even being picked up for a trial run as a weekend television show. Everything seemed to be falling into place, and as so often happens in life, this was exactly when God decided to show up with a different plan.

There was a seat open in Dad's congressional district and talk of him running for a third time. My parents had been discussing it for weeks, mulling it over, praying about it, and hadn't reached a decision. Considering Dad wins, could they give up their lives in Indiana? Sell the house they had built? Move away from their family and friends? Or would they risk it all to possibly lose the race yet again and be embarrassed a third time over?

They looked out at the view that day in 1999 and Mom took Dad's hand in hers.

Something caught her eye on the horizon, and she pointed to the sky. Dad's eyes followed and landed on two hawks flying far above them. They were gliding steadily on the wind's current, their wings still as they let the flow of air determine their path.

"If we're going to run again," she said, "then we're going to do it like those two hawks."

Dad looked back at her and she explained.

"No flapping," she said. "When we do it this time, we're going to let God carry us where He wants us to go without us trying to get there on our own."

And so it was decided.

No flapping.

Now here we are.

Let's begin.

Chapter Three

Answer the Call

I've seen many searching for answers far and wide . . .
For answers only you provide

—Chris Tomlin, "Good Good Father"

During the summer of 2016, I was working at a summer camp in Indiana. It was a traveling day camp where we descended upon a new church each week, unpacked, and set up supplies we used to engage the campers, including a rock wall, a giant swing, archery equipment, skit props, water slides, and more. We called ourselves "Vacation Bible School on steroids," and it was probably the hardest job I will ever have. God knew I needed to be surrounded by people who were following after Him in the summer leading up to campaign season.

The funny thing is, I almost didn't work so close to home. I had been accepted as a counselor at a camp in Canada and was planning on taking that job. One of my best friends was headed up there for the summer, too, and we were already talking about how much fun we were going to have. But something was telling me I shouldn't go. I can't explain it, even to this day, but I had a pit in my stomach, an aching feeling of dread. I couldn't figure out why. It was clearly the better option: It paid more, my friend was going to be there, it was a new adventure in a new country, but every time I thought of it, I couldn't shake the feeling it was wrong.

I had a couple days left before I needed to tell the camp directors which one I had chosen. I took a long walk down Lake Shore Drive in Chicago. It was cold, as it usually is, but I needed the wind, the turmoil, the rain. I put my headphones in and listened to "Good Good Father," a song one of my best friends had sent to me when I told her I needed some clarity. I listened to that song over and over again on the walk. I started to cry. I called Mom, and she told me to go to the doctor, and so I did and found out I had made myself physically ill from the stress, but it wouldn't go away.

I left the doctor with antibiotics in hand, walked back outside, and called Mom again. She talked me through it, told me it was so unlike me to get this worked up over a summer job—and she was right. Why was I freaking out about this clear choice? Canada was the better option in every way, but some force was pushing against me, telling me it was not.

A friend once told me that sometimes, no matter our religious beliefs, we seek out answers, we pray and ask God to show us the right direction, to make the way clear—and then, when He does, we don't believe it. He had made the choice clear for me. I didn't want to believe it.

I told the Canadian camp I had to decline their offer. I told my friend (still one of the most supportive people I know) and she understood. I graduated, packed up my car, drove down to Indiana, and moved in with my parents. I started working at a ministry camp in southern Indiana with no experience and no set plan for the future.

It astounds me when I look back and think about how my life would have been different if I had gone to the Canadian camp, if I had been in the wilderness, virtually unreachable, when Dad was chosen to be the vice presidential candidate for the Republican Party. I might have heard about it on television, or from a friend or a letter Mom would have written to me. I would have had to decide whether or not to leave and go back to the United States to join them. I wouldn't have been able to talk with them as much as I did and would have had no inkling of their thoughts.

I had no idea what the summer of 2016 was going to bring for our family, but something in the universe did and I am so glad I listened.

———— ∞ ————

It wasn't a formal event when my parents sat me down and told me Dad was being considered as the vice presidential running mate for Donald Trump, who was then the presumptive Republican presidential nominee. We were sitting on the front porch of Aynes House, the governor's cabin in Indiana. The Aynes House dates back to around the 1920s or 1930s and is named after the family that first lived there. It was acquired by the state of Indiana in 1939 and has been used by former Indiana governors as an Indiana version of Camp David. We used it a lot. Dad had been serving as governor for about three years, and during that time it was one of my parents' favorite places to go—a house just their size with a few bedrooms and a good backyard with a grill. After my morning run, I often came back to find them on the screened-in porch, with a Bible or book open, drinking coffee and catching up. I would first help myself to coffee and then join them outside to chat.

(In honesty, it's strange to me to be writing this in the past tense. It still feels like we'll go back there any moment now, and everything that has occurred since that morning in mid-June, 2016, has been a dream or a test or both.)

I sat down on that particular morning, and my parents were talking about something vaguely. I didn't often miss details of things happening that summer, since I was always around and up-to-date on the goings-on in the family—or so I thought. I asked what was up, and Dad turned to me and said he was being considered, along with a long list full of other well-qualified people, to be Donald Trump's running mate.

I don't know why, but I wasn't surprised. I hadn't been keeping up with the news that summer, as my job kept me busy all hours of the day and some of the night. I was living life like most busy people—away from the news, catching a few bits here and there in my off time or from the evening broadcasts with Lester Holt. I told Dad I wasn't shocked and that he would be a good pick.

He laughed, a little speechless, and commented how he was starting to think he was the only person in our family genuinely surprised by this news. He probably was. Maybe God just prepared us all in different ways, bringing the possibility to my mind every now and then. Maybe Dad was prepared because he hadn't considered it beforehand—perhaps that's how it needed to be for him.

I told Dad he would be a good vice president. I knew the implications of such a job, and I knew it was going to change our family forever, but for reasons I still don't know, I wasn't afraid. I had a sense of peace about it and knew if my parents felt they were being called to a position, they would follow.

And if called, before Dad could determine whether he should

accept the opportunity to be considered for service in the second-highest office of the United States, he needed to have answers to two questions. The first was what the job would entail and how he would be asked to define that historically ambiguous role. The second was a more personal request. He and Mom felt we would need to know the Trumps as a family in order to make a decision. Then our team got the message to the Trump team. We knew this second request was unlikely, since they were quite possibly the busiest family in the world at that time, and so we waited with low expectations.

To our surprise, we got a response quickly, and the Trumps invited us out to the Trump National Golf Club in Bedminster, New Jersey, to spend the weekend with Donald, Melania, and Barron. It was the weekend before July Fourth, and we hopped on a plane to fly out to the East Coast. I was the only Pence sibling available to go at the time, and I felt I was an ambassador of sorts. Family to family, I was the kid representative, and having never met any of the Trumps beforehand, I was able to have a fresh perspective.

When we arrived in Bedminster, we drove onto the grounds and I was unsure what to expect. It was a beautiful resort and golf course, and we spent time relaxing before I got a chance to meet the candidate himself. We carved time out of the day so that I could meet Trump, and what struck me the most was his kindness. Throughout the weekend, in multiple interactions, I saw it: I could tell he had a genuine heart and a desire to help people in the country.

After that weekend, we headed back to Indiana and would go on to discuss the events in the weeks to come. Mom and Dad decided that if an offer was made, they would accept. We were trusting God with whatever happened, and we felt blessed to have had the experiences we did up to that point.

When the offer for Dad to be Donald Trump's vice presidential running mate officially came in, it was a regular night. On the campaign trail, Dad retold the story to cheering crowds: "When the call came in the middle of the night, I said yes in a heartbeat!" It sounded like a good anecdote, a retelling that almost seemed embellished or made up, but it was true. It actually happened that way.

I sat on the couch, watching TV with my brother Michael's then-fiancée, now-wife, Sarah, and we waited. We knew a decision was going to come sometime soon, any day now, and whether or not we actively knew we were waiting for it on that specific night, something in the air felt significant.

Dad got word from one of his aides that someone was going to be calling, and when the phone rang, he took it downstairs in his office with Mom. Sarah and I glanced at each other. *Chopped* was playing in the background as moments passed. Dad and Mom came back into the living room and sat down on the couch. They were holding hands, and he asked me to get Audrey on the phone. Sarah called Michael.

With Audrey and Michael on speaker, all six of us huddled together around the phones. I fought the urge to yell, "Just tell us already!" and let Dad take in the moment.

"We wanted to tell you all together," he said, still holding Mom's hand, "and now we can." My siblings on the other side of the respective phone lines were silent.

He took a deep breath and went on. "Your dad was just asked to be the candidate for vice president of the United States." His voice caught with emotion at the end, and for a split second everyone took it in.

Then came the congratulations, the hugs, and the "I'm proud of you, Dad," from Michael, the marine, and from Audrey, the world traveler.

It was climactic, yet something about the moments after were, for lack of a better word, normal. We had gotten really big news, news that changed our lives, and yet, life went on. Sarah and I turned *Chopped* back on. I probably went to bed early because I was heading back to camp the next day. I may have slept heavily or not, I don't remember, but what I do know is life went on.

Chapter Four

Find Strength in Your Differences

We can't take any credit for our talents. It's how we use them that counts.

—Madeleine L'Engle, A Wrinkle in Time:
And Related Readings

My parents had three kids in three years. Beyond tending to the obvious onslaught of baby diapers during the first few years, that they managed having us so close together was an admirable feat that would impact our entire lives. Our proximity in age meant we went through the same things at the same time. This meant soccer teams, braces, school dances, and homecomings were all grouped relatively close together. While this must have been difficult for my parents at times, it is something for which I am most grateful. I was never without a sister, who was close enough in age to show me the ropes of fashion and attempt to introduce me to better music. I had a brother who braved middle school, high school, and college before me and followed his dreams first, convincing me by his fearlessness to follow mine.

I am sandwiched in the middle of these two amazing characters.

Michael is every bit of the quintessential big brother, and Audrey is the younger sister who is smarter, cooler, and taller than I am. This positioning made me into the person I am today, and these two people are my best friends. Growing up, their support, their challenges, and their questions kept me on my toes and gave me sure footing. It readied me for the challenges and excited me for the adventures that lay ahead.

A tried-and-true phrase in the Pence family household is "Climb your own mountain." This was originally used by my paternal grandfather and was passed on to us. I have turned to this advice many times in my life. It is not always the easiest path to follow—to forge your own way—but I have found it to be the most rewarding. My parents instilled this value in us at a young age by encouraging us to do our own thing—to find what we were good at, and what made us happy. I think this made my siblings and me even closer than we already were.

Since I was the only kid logistically able to travel on the campaign trail, I tried my best to play all parts of the Pence kids for Mom and Dad. I also tried to be the connection to normalcy for both my siblings and my parents. On either side of things during the election cycle—whether you were physically on the trail or connected virtually—much could easily get lost in translation. I knew I was the one who had a foot in both worlds. I wasn't the candidate or spouse, and yet, I also wasn't physically detached from the day-to-day. My personal relationships with my siblings was something that grounded me in the reality of my family during the campaign. Throughout my entire life, their personalities, strong sense of character, and differing opinions had prepared me for the tumult of any election cycle and created a version of myself ready to provide a new viewpoint whenever I could. Their strength gives me strength. Their confidence in me makes me more self-assured.

Sometimes they were able to join us on the trail for short periods of time, and it was always enjoyable. When my sister came along for a few days, I was reminded of campaigning with my siblings when we were little kids. I wrote about it in my journal at the time, saying it was "...perfect. Being able to show her everything, see her interact with Dad, and question him on topics...was all wonderful."

Together we retreated back to our little kid selves at fund-raisers and speeches given by our dad. We hung out with the staff backstage during his speeches, playing card games in the hold rooms. It reassured me of the fact that our family would always be who we are, and that was mainly due to the hard work of my parents spending time defining what our family is early on in our lives.

For me, the campaign trail became more real once Audrey was there with me, once we shared the experience together. With her, the life-changing events of that year became more than stories; they were memories we shared with one another. Our different perspectives added to the overarching story of that time that we are able to look back on and remember together. Having her perspective and sharing in the journey together influences me and gives me strength to face whatever may come in the future.

Throughout the campaign and after, I kept a journal. Journals have always been a method of therapy for me. They rarely take the form of one physical, organized booklet. Although that would have been easier to manage, it just isn't my style. No, I am the napkin-scribbler type, jotting notes on anything I can find in order to save them for later, the words and phrases I might need and will otherwise most certainly forget. On the campaign trail, I decided to keep such forms of journals, and so, over the course of that hundred-day journey, I kept track of small things that happened. Those words have contributed to this book, to this collection of

memories, and to this confiding in America. The first entry has
the following text at the top, and it sums up every day, every decision, and every action:

> I am trying to be a light. Like Despereaux: "Tell me a story.
> Make some light. Tell me a story."
> —My Campaign Trail Journal, July 2016

This was my motto for the campaign trail and everything the
year held for me and my family. We actively tried to live out this
idea. On the good days and hard days, on the hills and in the val-
leys, we just wanted to be a light. I hope we never lose sight of that,
even though it can be easy to do so.

Even during times when we're not physically together, we still
are; we're the same and we're different and that is what makes us
so close. As I wrote this book, I sent excerpts to Audrey, Michael,
and his wife, Sarah, as I made progress. I wanted their insight and
approval on what I was choosing to include. Audrey commented
to me one time that she could not imagine sitting down to write
an entire book. I thought about this. I am certain she would be
able to do this with ease, but what she meant was that it would be
uncomfortable for her. For me, this is easy and fun and good, but
she would rather have structure and set goals to accomplish rather
than an open-ended assignment like writing a book.

When I think of what she does for a living, though, I know I
would not find enjoyment or fulfillment in it. Not to mention, I
would be a terrible lawyer. Studying law would be interesting and
challenging for me, but the management, hours, and tasks of being
a lawyer would not suit my personality as well. As for my brother's job—a Marine Corps fighter pilot—we don't even need to go
there, but we will. I am not exaggerating when I say I could not do
what he does. My individual skills have never been on the side of

math and science and aeronautics. I could try, but I would not find the enjoyment in it that he does. He looks forward to flying every day. If he does not get to fly due to weather, he is noticeably down. This astounds me. If someone asked me to fly a plane, I would decline and accept a parachute before even attempting to learn.

I have the utmost respect for people like my brother who find it fun to enter into danger, and who feel it's their calling to translate this desire into acts of service in the military. He has been that way for as long as I can remember. He never passed on the potential for a thrill—whether it was riding a roller coaster, mountain biking, or snowboarding. I often followed him into dangerous situations only to come out of them much less intact, but always with a great story.

Once, when I was six years old, our family took a vacation to the beach. Michael spotted a dolphin in the ocean. Naturally, he told me we needed to chase the dolphin and we grabbed our noodles and ran out into the water. I felt a stabbing pain in my foot and it turned out I had stepped on a stingray and been stung. I have a very distinct memory of sitting on the edge of our bathtub in the hotel room, Mom on the phone with the doctor and Dad with his foot sticking into the hot water in solidarity with me, us soaking our feet to prevent infection. And Michael was right there, right behind me. I can still hear Mom saying to him, "Yes, read Charlotte a book. That's very nice, Michael," as he read me a story to distract me from the pain. No matter how the situation turned out, Michael was always there when I got hurt or things went wrong. He never asked me to come on an adventure without the unspoken assurance that he would take care of me.

Even in the childhood moments of mishaps and stung feet, there is a clear pattern, a method to the madness. Our personalities shone through at a very young age. While I always followed Michael around, Audrey would not have any of that nonsense.

As soon as she was born, she introduced a third opinion into the group. It was no longer a clear-cut yes or no. All of a sudden, there was a new person adding her personality to our adventures. Audrey was the one who taught me how to say no, how not to be a pushover, and how to stand up for myself in sticky situations. I still followed Michael around most of the time, but Audrey empowered me to think on my own. We started creating stories together where she would play along with my make-believe scenarios. One of our favorite games to play was the Mystery Game, where I would create a real-life Clue game and make up characters with evidence they had to uncover. Her friends played along and had to figure out the end of the story and solve the mystery. She was one of the first people to get me to tell my own stories and helped me find the self-assurance to do so.

The overwhelming differences in my siblings' personalities added dividends to the woman I have become. Though, I must admit, it is not lost on me I am equally as different. They encouraged and pushed me my entire life, but they also let me be my own person. It is inevitable that the middle child will take on some characteristics of his or her siblings. I could not be luckier to have these two as my examples, but the biggest impact they have had on me is encouraging me to branch out on my own. This led me to the campaign trail, to Washington, D.C., and out to Los Angeles. Although we are physically apart, the space between us is filled in with the knowledge that I need make only one call and they would both be by my side.

My parents never compared my siblings and me, and for that reason, we learned to encourage one another in our individual pursuits—even when we find ourselves separated by distance.

One thing my parents instilled in me specifically was the notion to never quit. We were encouraged to try new things and discover what we were good at instead of following what everyone else was doing. Once we started something, though, we were expected to see it through.

I remember when I was on the cross-country team in high school. After years of playing team sports that I enjoyed but wasn't passionate about, I discovered a love for running. And more than that—I discovered a skill. I was good at running, and I enjoyed it wholeheartedly.

The fall of my junior year of high school was busy, and I was scheduled to get my tonsils out halfway through the season. I went to a few meets but felt that it wasn't worth it for me to keep going. I knew things were going to pick up, and I didn't want to commit to the entire season. I let my parents know, and they said it was my decision whether to stay on the team. But I remember Dad was a little disappointed. He wasn't going to push me on it, but I could see it in his face.

"What?" I asked.

"I just don't think you should quit," he said.

I tried to reason with him, but really I was just trying to justify it to myself.

"There's no point, though. I'll only be able to do a few more meets—if that."

He shrugged. "You can do what you want. But you're not a quitter."

I sighed. He was right.

I finished out the season and continued track and cross-country the next few years. I continued to run throughout college, and I still run nearly every day.

Dad didn't push me to stay on the team. He let me decide, but he did challenge me, because he knew I was better than what I was allowing myself to do. He never wanted me to be on a sports team because Michael was, or to do more creative clubs like Audrey. He wanted me to do my best. That's all he ever asked, and by simply asking that, he made me demand it of myself.

In my family, we were encouraged to discover our own personalities and strengths and never look down on ourselves for not being good at something. If you aren't good at one thing, chances are, you are great at something else. If you need evidence, look no further than the Pence children, who have unsuccessfully attempted many sports teams, career paths, clubs, and societies in order to find what we are good at, as well as what we struggle with. Through this, we found what gave us life and passion.

My siblings and I are infinitely different, but we always celebrated these differences and this is what has made us so close in adulthood. My parents always encouraged us to compete against ourselves first, to be the best that we could be at any one thing no matter how well the person next to us was doing. It is this lesson I have carried with me that has helped me to realize my own dreams, to not compare those dreams to the ambitions of others, and to rejoice when I see others succeed.

Chapter Five

Speak Your Dreams

You can't very well find an answer to something if you do not first ask the question.

—My Campaign Trail Journal, August 2016

I n the moments following the Indiana gubernatorial election in 2012, my family was huddled in the bathroom of a suite. Minutes earlier, we had been surrounded by staffers, family, and close friends in a room at Lucas Oil Stadium, watching the results of the election roll in.

Dad had been down in the polls for about ten minutes, with the Democratic candidate leading by a few points. No one seemed to notice this as much as my immediate family, but we never took our eyes off of it as the tension grew. All around us, there was delicious catered food and drinks, but I distinctly remember I didn't touch any of it. There was a lot of commotion. People were taking pictures and excitedly grabbing me by the arm, saying, "Can you believe it? It's amazing!" And I thought to myself, "What exactly is so amazing?" We hadn't won yet and elections are anyone's game. You go out there for months, sometimes years, asking people to like you and trust you with their government, their state, or their country, and then you sit back and wait.

Someone I did very much enjoy talking to throughout the night was my paternal grandmother—Nini, as we grandkids call her. She was thoughtful, standing on the sidelines, watching the crowd of mostly people she could call family. She told me she was thinking about her late husband, my grandfather, and how he would have liked to be there. I told her he was there, in some way. I believe he was.

She smiled at me with a twinkle in her eye, knowing so much of life I cannot yet, and said, "Yes, he is. I know he is."

Dad spent a lot of time with her that night, too, and when the results were called, he gave her a big hug. She pulled him back with her arms out straight and looked him right in the face as I imagine she did so many times when he was a young boy, and said, "I'm proud of you." With tears in both their eyes, they embraced again, and I thought how special it is to have parents you wish to make proud. I know that feeling.

When the election was called and people left the room, the five of us needed to find a place where we could all regroup in private for a few minutes. The bathroom would do. The security personnel we would grow accustomed to in the years to come stood outside the door. We kids had decided to give our parents gifts. Mom did this after each election when we were growing up. There would always be some present, a memento, to thank us for what we had done—win or lose. This was planned from the start, and they hadn't expected it at all. Win or lose, we knew there was cause to celebrate our coming through an election and out the other side, still intact and still a family. It was something we had learned to do before and would again.

For Mom, we each wrote our favorite "Mom quote" from the campaign trail on a note card and framed them. They were all things she had said to us along the way, and they sum her up almost perfectly.

The three of them read as follows:

> *I'm not going to let what's going on out there affect what's going on in here.*
>
> *You teach your kids how to fight for their dreams by fighting for your own.*
>
> *I'm listening. And I hear you.*

Each of these sayings had been spoken to one of us at one point or another during Dad's campaign. Her words were relevant then, and they are now, too. The first is one of my favorites, and it was told to us when a certain media story was going around on the Internet. It was our first encounter with that awkward, uneasy feeling that people somewhere out there are talking about you without you there to defend yourself. We would attempt to get used to that feeling over the years as a family, but it is never a natural element to accept into your everyday life, and I am still not sure I have found the best way to cope with overhearing people talking about Dad via the Internet and media.

As we all sat in that bathroom awaiting the results of the gubernatorial election, Mom held the frame close to her when she first saw the words it housed. She read the phrases individually, her voice catching at the end of each. We hugged her, and thanked her, and I realized that her helpful words to us were now coming back to encourage her. The initial act of her speaking them aloud to us had come full circle, and now our acknowledgment of her attention and care was equally important, if not more so.

Mom would go on to reference this gift in a speech she gave as First Lady of Indiana. The subject of the speech, and the question she posed to the audience, was, "Who's on Your Stool?" The speech was about taking the opportunity to encourage others who need it when you have their attention, as Mom had encouraged us with her strength and wisdom during Dad's campaigns.

We have these two wooden stools that were staples throughout my childhood and teenage years. They are barstool height, old, and worn down. One has a bar missing across the middle, so when I try to set my foot on a rung, it just falls, getting me every time.

Countless evenings, I remember walking into the kitchen, taking a seat, and just observing whoever was around. It could have been Audrey doing a project at the kitchen table, or Michael making a snack after lacrosse practice. Most of the time, though, it was Mom.

She doesn't consider herself much of a cook, but in my opinion, she gives herself too little credit. In this memory, I want to think of her as making spaghetti because she made it all the time and it is amazing. Audrey and I have unsuccessfully tried to re-create it in our adult years (gluten-free for me now, as my diet has changed for health reasons).

Mom would have been stirring the spaghetti, adding the sauce into the saucepan on the stove next to it, and she would have waited while I sat. Whenever something specific was on my mind, she always knew, but she never pressed me to tell her. She waited until I was ready to bring it up to vent and talk it out, and she listened.

In her speech on this topic, Mom commented on the "stool conversations" we often had with her growing up. She said, "It's a special moment because it usually means we are engaged. They're talking, I'm listening. Or I'm talking, and they're listening. It's almost magical. I love it because in those moments, I'm not staring them in the eye. I am just present. They seem to be more free to talk. They can unburden themselves. . . . In those moments, God uses me, problems get solved, and life gets a little easier."

To this day, I still find myself on her stool at times, calling her during a lunch break or early in the morning on my way to work, since living in different time zones makes communication difficult. While she is still always there for me, I struggle now as an adult to recognize who is "on my stool." Whom do I need to chat to, listen to, or simply spend time near, in order for them to feel comfortable opening up to me when they are ready? It might be a coworker, a sister, or a friend sitting there, waiting for someone who is not too busy to listen.

Mom went on in her speech to talk about that very election night in 2012 when Dad became governor. She pulled out the framed quotes we had given her in the bathroom, containing each of her sayings. She said, "It is probably the greatest gift I have ever been given or will ever get in my entire life."

The opportunity to encourage people doesn't always come in a physical, in-person conversation. People let us know they need encouragement in the most discreet of ways sometimes, but we are always able to notice if we pay close enough attention.

Motherly advice comes to me in many forms in my life, including hidden notes stuffed away in the bottom of a bag, in between clothes or as pocket stowaways. I take them out, immediately knowing what they are, and read their words. This is something Mom often does when I move to a new place or set out on a different adventure. I want to keep them, hold on to them forever, but I know their true value is experienced in the moment I see them. She never tells me they are there. She just waits for me to find them on my own; there is some intentionality about this, I know. She trusts they will be revealed to me when I need them the most.

When I left to study abroad in England for my junior year of college, Mom gave me a necklace of a tiny book with little pages inside of it. I wore it at times and hung it up on the shelves in my dorm room when I wasn't wearing it, but it wasn't until I was packing up my belongings to leave that I noticed it wasn't just a necklace. It was a love note from her with words written in the form of a long note.

She could only fit a few words on each of the tiny pages, but as I turned them, the entire book read one long sentiment:

Dear Booh,
    We believe in you!
    Go climb your mountain.
    Discover God's best for you.
    Love,
    Mom and Dad
    9.10.14

All that time, I had never known that around my neck, I carried not only a memento she had given me, but also her words hung there, too. I think somehow, in some way, they sustained me during that year and gave me strength without my knowing it. If I had found them earlier, maybe her advice would have given me encouragement in my days of homesickness abroad. They may have helped me feel closer to home, but I don't like thinking that way. I believe I was meant to find them at the end of my journey instead of while I was on it. They reminded me of the home to which I was returning and the love of a family I had never really left.

I still have that necklace in my apartment in Los Angeles. It hangs on my wall alongside other pieces of jewelry. I know whenever I lose faith in myself, I can find evidence of her faith in me there.

On the 2016 campaign trail, I saw Dad instill faith in a lot of people. I witnessed as he spoke words of encouragement to many of those we met. Some of my favorite moments involved kids. Children of all ages would come up to shake his hand, dressed in their Sunday best, with nervous parents gently nudging them into position from behind in order to snap a picture.

One moment in particular happened backstage at a rally in Iowa. A girl in the sixth grade wearing a nice blue dress, her hair pulled back in a braid, waited patiently with her family in the photo line. When it was their turn, her mom scooted everybody together and told her little ones to shake Dad's hand. Dad leaned down, asked each of their names, and commented on how nice they all looked.

The girl's dad pointed to her and proudly exclaimed, "She's her class representative!"

She was shy and didn't appear to want a lot of attention drawn to this fact.

Dad then asked her if she wanted to go into politics, to which she nodded hesitantly.

"That's the first step," he encouraged. "Admitting it. I always tell young people who want to go into politics to say it—tell people. Speak your dreams. That's the first step. So great job."

She blushed, thanked him, and smiled for the picture.

He pointed at her as they walked away and said, "I'll be keeping an eye out for your name on a ballot."

Her parents thanked him sincerely and walked away, looking over their picture.

During his rally speech later, my mind wandered to that little girl and the advice he had given her, and given me over the years.

Speak your dreams.

It might be the hardest part of doing or starting anything, to admit the desire exists. Criticism and opposition will always come when we first set out, but the hardest part is admitting to ourselves, and to others, that we have a calling we must follow.

I have felt this way before in regard to writing. It is something I feel most natural while doing, yet admitting to people that you love to write can be somewhat of a conversation killer, and I got tired of adults looking at me with a glance that said, *Oh, your poor parents.*

I don't know many parents who encourage their children to go to film school and also to get a "backup" major in creative writing, but mine did, and when I didn't have the courage or the will to speak my dreams, they were there to help.

Dad has always said to me, "You're my writer, Charlotte," and even though I didn't believe him at times, he kept on believing. Mom likes to tell the story of my two-year-old self sitting on a chair, turning pages in a book I couldn't read yet, just taking in the symbols that made up the words I didn't understand. I was fascinated by stories from a young age, and even before I could write, I remember scribbling on pages, pretending to fill a book with events that existed in my head.

There is something powerful about saying things out loud, declarations we may think other people don't want to hear. But really, we are the ones who perhaps don't want to hear them, don't want to be reminded of our dreams because the potential for failure scares us. It can be easier to push dreams aside, but it is ultimately defeating.

Chapter Six

Enjoy the Ride

*The credit belongs to the man who is actually in the arena . . . who
at the best knows in the end the triumph of high achievement, and
who at the worst, if he fails, at least fails while daring greatly, so that
his place shall never be with those cold and timid souls who neither
know victory nor defeat.*

—*Teddy Roosevelt*, The Man in the Arena;
excerpt from the speech "Citizenship in a Republic"

The night Dad became governor of Indiana, after we had
exchanged our gifts in that bathroom, there was a victory rally in the field area of the stadium. We went over,
walking out through the tunnel and onto the field, where a massive
stage had been put up. Media gathered and as we walked out into
the lights, with people cheering and friends and family reaching
forward to shake our hands and congratulate us, I noticed my parents, as always, holding hands. I turned around and eyed my siblings, who looked just as bewildered as I felt. I reached out my hand
and grabbed ahold of Audrey's, who linked arms with our brother,
and we all walked out together, just as we had entered that race

and would enter many stages in the future. We walked out into the spotlight and the five of us raised our hands in victory. Then we went home.

We had moved back to Indiana from D.C. earlier that summer and rented a house in the suburbs. A few months earlier, I had gone to Chicago to start as a freshman at DePaul University, taking the Megabus down to Indianapolis for big campaign events—and election night, of course.

Later that night, I watched more coverage of the election in our living room. Obama won a second term, beating Mitt Romney and Paul Ryan. I got congratulatory texts about Dad's win from many friends, some of whom I would not hear from even after the national 2016 election just four short years away. Dad watched TV with me as the night wore on, and he asked me how I was doing. I said I was fine, knowing that most of the friends I had met in college so far didn't know who the governor of Indiana was—and didn't much care. I was sometimes nervous that my last name would be recognized, but oh how little did I know then.

As Dad headed upstairs to call it a night, he stopped on the first step, looked directly at me, and gestured to the news coverage still playing in the background.

He said, "Everything has changed, and nothing has changed."

How I would go on to cling to those words.

After he was gone, I considered what he said and whether or not he was right. Everything *had* changed. Things were going to be different now. We were officially back in Indiana—a place I had always considered home yet I had not spent the majority of my years growing up there. I was going back to Chicago for school, where I was still trying to make new friends in my first year, and I feared that people might start to treat me differently.

My sister was moving to Indiana to finish her senior year of high school, and now Michael, having gone to Purdue, was suddenly a lot more notable—his name being the same as the new governor. Things were changing, but our family was still the same. We were still us and I knew that much of what he meant was true.

As time went on, I realized it didn't matter as much whether or not what Dad said was true. We had no way of knowing what challenges lay ahead for the Pences in our parents' newfound roles. Surely he understood best how much really *had* changed and would continue to change. Yet, still, he said it because he knew what mattered most in that moment was his willingness to say it and my need to hear it. He spoke aloud that promise and I knew he meant it. That was all I needed to know.

I came to learn the smallest changes were the hardest to get used to. Taking time to enjoy the little changes and keep a positive perspective, and a sense of humor about the situation, helps me with any transition I find myself in.

This lesson for me started when Dad became governor and continued when he became vice president. The day after Dad's official acceptance speech for the candidacy of the vice president, I wrote the following in my campaign trail journal:

> *Secret Service started today. They do not like revolving doors.*
> *Honestly, who does?*
> —July 19, 2016, Cleveland, Ohio

Reading back over my journal, I laughed aloud at this, but there is truth in the sentiment behind it. I was learning the whole way, and continually surprised at the new things I learned. The lack of privacy and constant presence of protective detail are aspects I heard about, yet I didn't realize the level of adjustment that comes with it. It is a privilege and honor to be protected by individuals who spend time away from their families and risk their lives in order to protect my family. It is truly humbling, but it takes some getting used to and I am not sure I will ever be fully "used to" it.

Dad and I haven't ridden in a car alone together in six years. When I was a kid, I remember taking drives with him to run errands or just get out of the house for a while. It didn't matter where he was going; I just wanted to be there. When we were back in Indiana, we would roll down the windows, smell the fresh air of the cornfields, and blast country music down two-lane roads. One of his favorite places to go was Thorntons gas station, which is still there, by the way. He loved stopping in to talk with the cashier, a kind, older woman who would tell it to him straight. He always calls clerks and cashiers by the names on their badges. When I was a teenager, it used to bug me that he was making such a *point* to do it. I gave him a hard time about it once, teasing him to stop acting all buddy-buddy with random strangers, and he looked at me with a serious face and said, "Why do you think they wear name tags, Charlotte?" He was right, and I was wrong—not for the first time, or the last.

Dad always got a couple of Cokes for us, and maybe some M&M's for Mom, and we would hop back into the truck and be on our way. I don't think he even had a route when we would take those drives. He just liked going with no plan and no backup plan.

He told me stories when we drove together, stories about his childhood and how he used to take drives with his dad, too, when he was my age. Sometimes, when we were back in Columbus, he would get an idea in his head about somewhere he needed to show me and we would take a random turn and find ourselves in a different neighborhood, unrecognizable to me. One time in particular, he slowed down, turned toward the curb, and stopped in front of a white house.

"There it is," he said with a look in his eye. "The White Whale."

"Excuse me?"

"The house my parents bought when we all moved out."

He pointed to the front door. "Right there was where I brought your mom home to meet my family for the first time." He paused as his voice caught with emotion. I knew he was remembering his dad.

I looked back at his face as he spoke. In that front yard, he saw a scene he had lived before, one I couldn't see and was only able to feel and infer from him. We turned down the road again after that, out into another memory, maybe even to make a new one this time.

The last time we rode in a car together was after the Indiana gubernatorial election. I remember it well, because I was driving that time, and we were headed back to my college in Chicago. Dad gave me the advice he always gave us: his "rule of three things." He listed them off on his fingers: faith, studies, and health. His unchanging philosophy behind this advice is pretty simple. He contends that if you make a point every day to spend time focused on those three things, everything else will fall into place.

If you take time for your faith, whether it is through devotions, prayer, or fellowship with other people, and keep up with your education and stay healthy, then the rest of the stressful factors of college will come together. As an adolescent and young adult (and, frankly, as an adult, too), it is easy to get distracted by the need to socialize or find a career path or enter into a relationship. We can let these things detract from the everyday importance of making time for God and making time for ourselves. My siblings could recite this advice back to you, since we have all been given it time and time again.

On that particular car ride, it was nighttime on I-65 north from Indianapolis to Chicago, and we saw the windmills. These aren't the tiny windmills you see in cartoons with cottages and horses. These are massive, and at night they are especially terrifying. For miles, the final stretch of that trip, as far as we could see in every direction, were the red lights that flash to warn planes. As the arms of the windmills spin, collecting energy, the red lights seem to blink at you—like an army of Martians.

I glanced at him in the passenger seat next to me, the country music radio playing softly in the background. I realized we were both entering into unknown seasons of our lives with me in my freshman year of college and him taking on the new major role of governor. We were going into our situations blindly, hoping our instincts, our family, and our faith would sustain us. We were both nervous.

"You're going to be a good governor," I said.

"I'm going to do my best," he said.

"You will be."

"And how do you know?"

"Because you're a good dad."

I drive alone a lot now. I still play country music, no matter what state, country, or time zone I am in. Sometimes, I glance at the passenger seat, find it empty, and smile to myself as a memory finds its way back into my mind.

I don't know if I will ever ride in a car alone with Dad again. I have come to terms with the fact that I cannot plan the future. I can't rely on my desires for new memories to be made because there is no backup plan in life—as much as we may convince ourselves there is.

Maybe one day we will take another ride together and we will blast Kenny Chesney and Garth Brooks down two-lane roads and we will go nowhere and everywhere, but maybe not. Until then, we will embrace this road we find ourselves on, we will embrace each other, and we will enjoy the ride.

Chapter Seven

Trust the Grand Plan

And we would have had to grab at it, make sure it was real,
hold on tight, and not let go . . .
opened our eyes, looked around, and stuttered a little
before we realized we had made it through.
Just where we end up, we don't know yet,
on this other side of the chasm.

—My Campaign Trail Journal, October 2016

W hen we went to New York City for the official announcement that Dad had been chosen as Donald Trump's running mate, our trip began a bit unusually. Before we left, we stowed away in the backseat of a car while decoys were dispatched to throw off the press outside our home. It was still a secret that Dad was the choice, and we didn't want it to get out ahead of it being officially announced. The press had been staking out our house for a few days. I waved to them on my morning runs as they panned their cameras toward me. Our neighbors let them use their driveways, and I wouldn't be surprised if a few home-cooked meals were offered to them in that famous, hospitable Hoosier way. They were eager to get in on the secret, but the truth is, nobody knew outside of our immediate family—not even my cousins or my grandmother were able to know.

We hunched down in our seats and headed to the airport, boarded a private plane, and took off for New York. I was absolutely loving it. All of my pretend runaway attempts as a kid had paid off in this moment. I remember looking at Dad and Mom, hiding their faces as we passed the cameras outside, holding hands, and giggling to each other.

To be honest, I am not sure exactly what I was thinking at that moment. I was certainly having fun, and I was along for the ride no matter what was ahead. The three of us, we were in it together. As we drove away and left Indiana, I knew that when we set foot back in our home state, things would never be the same, and I felt a sense of peace. Something about the whole process—from this very beginning, throughout the campaign trail, and right up to election night, no matter what the result would be—I had no doubt it was going to be okay. It was where we were supposed to be.

When we landed in New York City, two helicopters followed our car all the way to the hotel where we were staying. A mob of reporters gathered outside, and I remember clinging to the edge of Dad's suit coat so as not to get dragged behind with the crowd. I had never fully appreciated how intimidating paparazzi can be, but I will never again doubt celebrities who speak of their negative experiences being followed and photographed.

That night, a terrorist attack took place in Paris and the official announcement of Dad being the pick was postponed, so Trump put out a tweet in his famous fashion, stating he had picked Dad. I still have a picture of Dad holding up the tweet on his phone, hugging Mom, tears in both of their eyes. That's when things felt real.

We were pretty much quarantined in our hotel room before the announcement, since press surrounded the hotel outside. A few days later, once the press conference had been held and all was said and done, we got back on a plane and headed to Indiana. We landed to a rally in the airport's hangar with friends and family standing in the cold to cheer us on as the plane taxied to meet them. Dad gave a short speech thanking everyone, and we headed home and got to work.

We were in election season now and as any political kid knows, it was go time.

When the news had broken earlier that Dad was going to be the pick, he called his mom, who was watching our car being followed on TV in New York. I heard her on the other end of the line say, "Michael? Is it true?" and they both broke down in tears. He got calls from his brothers and sisters, all congratulating him, telling him he had earned it, and this was the culmination of a lifetime of public service. He was overwhelmed, humbled, and grateful for this chance to serve his country.

As he would go on to tell folks for months to come, when people had asked if he would consider saying yes to the offer of being a vice presidential candidate, he thought of members of the military—one of them being his late father, who had served in Korea.

He said, "I have always believed that this is a country I would give up my life for. So, if the question is, 'Would I give up my job for it?' then the answer is yes."

Dad never served in the armed forces. He would name it as his one regret in life, if he were asked. The members of the military who sacrifice so much for our safety and ability to live in peace are the true heroes of this story—and every story of America. They deserve the praise, the recognition.

And if any of you service members or your loved ones find yourselves as readers of this book, I hope you know you are seen and appreciated.

No sacrifices my family has made, no criticisms we have

received, or hardships we have endured are anything compared to what you go through each day.

So, thank you.

Forever, thank you.

———— ∞∞ ————

There was another, much more sobering trip to New York City than the one we left Indiana for. The first time Dad ever visited the city was the week after the attacks on September 11, 2001.

He went to Ground Zero.

On 9/11, I remember being scared because my second-grade self knew bad things were happening in D.C., and that was where my dad worked and we lived nearby. When he decided to go to Ground Zero to see the place where the Twin Towers had once stood, just one week after they had fallen to terrorists, it terrified me.

I remember every day on the way to school driving past the Pentagon with the big, black hole in it. It was a reminder of the evils of the world, but also the resilience. A giant American flag was hung right after the attack; it stayed up for a month and then came down, revealing the damage underneath. The American spirit of the flag was still felt where it had hung—and it felt like the perseverance of freedom in the face of evil.

My parents have a saying and it goes like this: "The safest place in the world is to be in the center of God's will," and whenever they say it, they hold their hand out, palm up, and point right to the middle.

This always led me to picture God's will as something tangible, something I could feel all around me, and truthfully, there have been many times in my life when I have. Sometimes, though, it can be easier to ignore this advice. It can be easy to think there are things we can do to make ourselves live in safety and peace without anything bad ever happening. Similarly, it can be easy to live in constant fear and think that no matter what we do, God won't be there—to buy into the lie that there is no force looking out for us or guiding our way.

I think what my parents mean when they say this is that whatever happens, happens. There are tragedies that can be prevented, and there are some that can't, and maybe the best way to cope with the unexplainable sadness that occurs in this world is to do everything we can to trust we are at the center of something bigger, a grand plan.

It can be the hardest thing to do, but if we follow the path we believe we have been set on for a specific purpose, then we have to trust that it is the right one. No matter what may lie ahead.

Chapter Eight

Value Connection

*Watching Dad's Town Hall today was interesting. I watched the
people's faces as he spoke. I watched the children that had come
out, all dressed up, to hear what he had to say. The people who
talked and called out, "Yes" and "Go on, now" when he would
say something inspiring. The way the room fell silent from shouting
and applauding when he would quiet his voice and get serious for a
moment . . .*

—My Campaign Trail Journal, August 2016

The campaign trail forced me to examine the power of connection with others. During my family's trip across America, I was pushed outside of my bubble and was reminded how to balance constant interaction with the necessity of alone time. One particular way I saw the power of human relationships was through my dad's interactions with real people, the constituents, and everyday Americans. He was able to engage with people at a variety of local stops, from county fairs to, you guessed it, town halls.

I observed town halls to be some of Dad's favorite events. They were where he exceled the most, where his character and demeanor showed through. He loved these events, where the public came together to hear him give his speech—the "stump speech," as it is called. He typically gave the same one at every stop, varying it slightly based on the room he was in or the state we were visiting at the time. Current events and the media changed the direction of the speech at times, too.

Dad always asked members of the armed forces to stand or raise their hand to indicate they had served in the military. The crowd would applaud them, often giving a standing ovation. He also thanked the police officers and members of law enforcement in attendance. This included our Secret Service personnel, who would try not to break a smile as citizens looked them in the eyes and clapped, mouthing "Thank you" to the nearest agent.

At town halls, Dad gave a shorter version of his rally speech; then he took questions from the crowd. People asked the same things no matter what state we were in. They asked about Donald Trump; they asked about health care, Social Security, and VA benefits. They told Dad they were praying for him. The people who came out to these events were supporters, but they were also skeptics. They wanted us to earn their vote, and that was why we went.

Along with meeting voters, another important part of attending town halls was giving encouragement to the volunteers who orchestrated these events. We often stopped by GOP headquarters in various cities to thank the teams. We had to surprise them, since we weren't allowed to announce where we were going ahead of time for security reasons. These visits were always fun; people excitedly took pictures and shook Dad's hand, after he gave a pump-up speech to thank them for all they did.

We visited one of the GOP headquarters under less enthusiastic conditions. The Trump–Pence headquarters of Orange County, North Carolina, was attacked about halfway through the campaign trail. We stopped at the headquarters and saw the burnt interior of the building. A handmade explosive device was thrown through the window and the couch was entirely charred. One of the men working there told us he had slept on the couch many times but had decided against it for whatever reason that night. If he had been there, he would have been seriously injured, if not killed.

We surveyed the damage, including spray-painted messages on the side of the building, declaring, "Nazi Republicans Leave Town or Else."

The volunteers there showed us the damaged signs and supplies in various rooms. Dad made comments to the press afterward and comforted the people there. It was clear they were scared and shaken. The small town of Hillsborough, North Carolina, woke up one morning to a much different reality. They were suddenly the center of a tragedy, and the country focused its full attention there for a moment. Our visiting them also brought attention, which at times can feel strange to do, but I think it is still important. Mom and Dad often spend time visiting people who have gone through a disaster—whether natural or man-made. Showing up for people who have gone through a tragedy is part of serving in public life. Sometimes I feel helpless doing this, but it's still important to simply let people know their leaders are present and that they see them. In this case, we were there mainly to encourage the survivors and to condemn the evil they had experienced.

I hope we were able to uplift them, to share in the human connection of their experience. Maybe the only thing we can try to do is be the light in the shadows, the hope in the midst of fear.

My interactions with people on the trail ultimately reminded me of the good in humanity and helped me to recognize the power of people connecting with one another. Campaign trails are packed with people. Not only was I able to meet new people who were supporters, but I also interacted with our entire team on a daily basis. For an introvert like myself, it took a bit of getting used to.

Soon after the Republican National Convention, our security detail increased dramatically and we had more staff than ever coordinating our every move and planning out the most minute details of our schedule. I remember actively reminding myself to spend time alone, which I rarely had the chance to do. When I started feeling overwhelmed or claustrophobic, I took a moment to myself—wherever I could get it—and reminded myself to breathe. I also dove into books on the trail and read as many as I could. I kept a running list of what I was reading and sometimes posted pictures of my "book club." I never travel without a few books on hand, and the trail gave me the perfect excuse to bring as many along as I could fit in my luggage. I even had a quote in a note on my phone about the importance of packing books. It read:

> When packing, always sacrifice clothes for books. Books don't care what you look like, so surely you won't need that extra shirt or pair of shoes.
>
> —Katarina Bivald

Reading wasn't simply a way to pass the time. It was the fulfillment of a desire to enter another world and expand my horizons, while my physical existence was confined to planes, cars, and hotel rooms for months. I understood the power of books before that experience, but I never felt it as much as I did then. Reading and taking time to myself were key on the campaign trail, where I relied upon my introverted nature when needed.

Ironically, the same journey also plopped me right down into a scenario where I was not going to be alone very often—physically or mentally—and it gave me the perception that people were watching my every move. Even though this may not have been the case, the feeling of it could be just as debilitating as if it were reality.

But I learned to embrace the learning experiences along with the potentially challenging moments. All we can do at the end of the day is learn how to best be ourselves and celebrate every corner of our being. We have to take care of that self, but we also have to acknowledge the self in every other person. Instead of fretting over how we are getting along with our fellow humans, we should be eager to enter into every situation with the intent to leave that person in better spirits. It may seem like this is impossible, since sometimes we have to be the bearers of bad news or reprimand someone for something they did. However, I believe negative encounters don't have to leave negativity in their wake.

It reminds me of a motto Dad often says, and one I had printed on a canvas for him as a gift once: "Do the right thing," he says. "Then go home for dinner."

Make the right decision as you believe it to be in the moment, and treat people with respect and kindness. Then call it a day. Go home. Have dinner with your family and do something else other than allowing the weight of the world to cave in on you, because it can.

It can for all of us.

After Dad was elected, I felt a strange weight on me. The attention his new position drew to our family impacted the way I was able to connect with some people because of unexpected expectations. It wasn't because I was famous or recognized on the street. I wasn't, and I'm still not. I definitely don't consider myself to be famous, but some people—even some I had existing relationships with—suddenly seemed to try something on every time they spoke to me. They wanted to know more about the family of one who serves the upper levels of the United States government. Maybe they thought it would help them understand better who Mike Pence was, if they could get to know his daughter and form an opinion about her.

I felt as if every interaction I had needed to be perfect. I felt people looking at me in restaurants when I went out with family friends who told the waiters who I was. I tried to be as polite and kind as I could be, so they wouldn't have any less faith in my family after meeting me. At first, it was a lot of pressure and as imperfect of a person as I am, I didn't think I was up to the challenge. I realized over time that although it felt like a burden to be responsible for people's perceptions of my parents, it was actually a good thing, a blessing. As many situations that originate as hardships often become, it was an opportunity. I was able to provide context for people curious about my family and our daily lives.

I discussed this concept with friends at the time. They felt bad for me and said it was unfair for people to jump to conclusions or judge my family based on an average encounter with me. They said it was different for people who have the advantage of inconspicuousness and can treat others however they want because they don't have a famous last name.

While I appreciated my friends' concern, I thought about this a lot. I decided that even though it felt strange to have a higher standard to live up to, maybe I should have always acted in that way, being intentional about my actions and the way I engage with people, even before my last name was anything of note. Maybe, without knowing it, I had not been as thoughtful of my actions as I should have been. This concept can apply to everyone, and it applied to me even before my family went through this experience. We all have the capability to impact someone's day in a positive or negative way. We are all being watched, even if we don't think our actions matter.

A few weeks into the campaign trail, at a Trump–Pence rally in Denver, Colorado, I noticed a young man in the crowd who was wearing a suit but who couldn't have been older than ten or eleven. He leapt to his feet whenever the audience applauded and came up to meet my dad afterward. Later on that same day, at a town hall, I saw a little girl with red, white, and blue ribbons in her hair, sitting beside her mother. Her mother guided her through the crowd and to the front of the rope line so that she would be able to shake my dad's hand. The experience struck me, and I wrote about it in my *Glamour* magazine article, "Mike Pence's Daughter Reveals the Lessons Her Father Taught Her." I said, "Watching the way these kids looked up at my dad as he spoke, with such admiration and hope in their eyes, reminded me that it doesn't matter where we are in life—we're always being observed."*

When this concept was still new to me in the early days after the campaign, I felt a bit awkward. As a proud introvert, this was hard for me, but I have become more comfortable with it over time. It is certainly easier for me to keep to myself. While I am

---

* Glamour.com, "Mike Pence's Daughter Reveals the Lessons Her Father Taught Her," Charlotte Pence, October 4, 2016, accessed March 2018. https://www.glamour.com/story/charlotte-pence-small-actions-matter

proud of this personality trait and have learned to love it, it can also be used as a crutch. I believe in pushing myself outside of my comfort zone, and challenging my tendency to spend time alone is a key way to do so. The campaign trail, therefore, was a perfect testing ground.

Chapter Nine

Keep the Circle

There will always be things that we can learn from one another.
—My Campaign Trail Journal, July 2016

To remind you of how quickly things moved after Dad was selected as a candidate for the vice presidency, there were only two days between when Donald Trump formally announced he was picking Dad, on July 16, 2016, and the Republican National Convention, on July 18, 2016. The day after Dad was announced, a few speechwriters came to him with a draft of his convention speech, but he completely reworked it. He sat down with them for many sessions, wanting it to be in his voice. This was the first impression he would be making on the nation and the world—not to mention the first time he'd share his opinion of his running mate. Officially speaking, it was also his acceptance of this massive honor, and Dad was intent on getting it right.

He practiced the speech for me in the hotel room the night before the convention, making last-minute edits that would appear on the teleprompter the next day. He allowed me to comb through it, checking for errors or repetitions, and I read through it many times over. I continued to review Dad's speeches while we traveled on the campaign trail. After every rally speech, he asked me how he had done and if he should change any of the wording or delivery. I took notes and gave him feedback on plane rides in between events. Over time, I came to realize why he did this. He would tell you it was helpful to him, since I am a writer and was not the speaker and was able to listen to the speeches with a somewhat detached point of view. I think he did it for me, though. He knew I needed a job, a reason to feel important and valued on the trail, and this was my contribution.

Along the campaign, I heard Dad make remarks and give pieces of advice. One of them was, "Everyone is under-encouraged." Meanwhile, in his own job, he took every opportunity to tell people they were doing well at their jobs. He did so with his own staff, with me, and with workers and business owners we met in the states we visited. Of course, he suffers from the typical Midwestern style of being overly humble when it comes to himself, but when talking about others, he never shies away from saying how well they do what they do—even when they have recently messed up. Actually, no, make that *especially* when they have messed up. He's right about this. People need more encouragement and inclusion. It is not natural to feel part of the group as a human. Oftentimes those with strong opinions feel very much on the outside. When we bring people together, even if they may be from opposite positions, it is ultimately gratifying and beneficial to society.

In my family, we often refer to ourselves as a circle. We protect one another, and we keep our private lives inside the circle, but once you are on the inside, you are never out. You are a part of our lives forever. When Michael and Sarah got engaged, she entered the circle, and she handles all of these experiences with extraordinary grace. Our lives have continued to be especially eventful since the time Sarah entered the fold.

The day before the Republican National Convention was Sarah's birthday. She and Michael would be in attendance for the event. Mom and I made a quick run to a local grocery store in Cleveland to buy balloons, cookies, cake, and confetti to decorate her room. We paid for our mini-party supplies, and then went out to the Secret Service vehicles, only to realize we had a problem. The balloons would not fit in the back of the car, since these vehicles are armored and have a different skeleton than regular cars. We stuffed them into the "trunk" and did our best not to laugh as the agents stood around us, unable to help, as they are required to have their hands free at all times.

The entire ride back to the hotel, I noticed the streets of Cleveland were mostly empty due to the increased security on the borders of the city. It was extremely difficult for anyone to enter during the convention since security was very tight. Despite this eeriness I felt along the vacant roads back to the hotel, I couldn't help but smile to myself as one of the balloons we had bought loudly played "Happy Birthday." Every time it bumped up against the ceiling, the song began again, and the ridiculousness of our situation began to set in. Here we were, just a normal family in our eyes, heading to surprise our (almost) sister-in-law with a birthday celebration. Yet, we were in cars similar to tanks being driven by people we did not know through a city that had been all but closed down due to the presence of, among other important people, us. It was odd.

So is the life of a political family. I am someone who loves stories and welcomes any chance to put myself in an odd situation to get a story out of it. It is uncomfortable at times, but when we go into these strange situations flanked by the people whom we care about most, it is fun and inspiring.

The stories, the people, and the life lessons I've been impacted by are shared in this book to help shed light on current situations—whether in your life or in the world. We always have the possibility to better ourselves and continue to grow and adapt as life changes.

Dad teaches me to adapt every day by adjusting to new challenges as they come his way. His days are fairly unpredictable, and he never lets stress or changes in schedule affect how he treats other people. Through his actions, he reminds me to welcome the uncertain avenues of life and to do so with patience. I see this in the way he treats everyone around him, including those closest—us, his family.

At times, it can be easier to allow our own presumptions to get in the way of our potential for positive growth. Instead of welcoming a new situation, we may want to hide away. I would challenge you, the reader, to step toward those moments that cause insecurity, because in doing so, you may just be surprised by the people you find there.

People often ask me about how it is to work in the entertainment industry with a father in politics. It is a question and concern I may have never faced if Dad were not serving in his current position. This is the reality I live in now, though, and so as with other unforeseen situations, I have adapted and learned how to find the lesson in my interactions. And through it all, the inner circle continues to be my support system. My family members will always come first for me, and when I find myself in a new environment faced with unknown challenges, they are the ones I can always find right beside me.

In regards to working in entertainment as a "Pence," the truth is, I don't think about it very often. Politics is just my dad's job, and I don't want to assume other people allow their presuppositions about me to determine how we interact.

In a very different job, I once had to prove myself in another way. In my coming-of-age summer, after my freshman year at college, I worked at a horse barn in southern Indiana. It was in Brown County State Park, where the governor's cabin is located. I had an internship at the PBS affiliate in Indianapolis during the week, but I needed a job for when we went down south on the weekends. We pulled up to the place where a cowboy character owned a barn, which he ran trail rides out of with his wife and three young daughters.

I had short, cropped hair and a blond streak through my bangs. I walked up in boots that still needed to be broken in. He let me know those would not work, that I would have blisters on my feet by the end of the day. He was right. It took me a few days to get comfortable there and my body ached each night. I had grown up riding horses sporadically, but I had never been around them this much. Every day I shoveled horse manure, mulch, and gravel from early in the morning to late at night. I fed the horses in the morning, saddled and bridled them, then let them free to run in the nearby pasture at the end of the day. That was my favorite part.

When the last trail rides finished, we cleaned the barn out and removed the bridles and saddles from the horses. They could smell their freedom then. I led them through a small creek to the edge of the gate where the open field lay ahead. They picked up speed and there was no stopping them once I cracked the gate open, letting them roam freely for the remainder of the evening. I can still see those horses running for the sunset.

I must have been a sight to see that summer. The other people working there knew I was the governor's kid. Maybe they expected someone a bit more polished. Maybe they thought I would burn out before the end of the season. I don't think so, though. I think they just waited to see how I would do, on my own merit, in my own way. They gave me a chance and didn't treat me any differently than the other people working there. I did every job expected of me to the best of my ability, and that is how I have tried to act in every job I have had since.

We each experience these situations at some point. When people make assumptions about us, debunking them can be fun if we let it be. It certainly has been for me. Entering into these scenarios, where you're misperceived and have the opportunity to prove yourself, can be intimidating, but it is also important to do it. If we simply keep to ourselves, then we allow assumptions to run rampant without disproving them through conversation or otherwise. This can be especially true within families.

When the campaign trail officially started, our family circle would be tested like never before. We would have to stay connected even when it was hard, even when we disagreed. We were not immune to the divisiveness the election brought out in people. We worked through it by talking and not shying away from controversy. We had to, and we came out on the other side, ready to face the next steps together. About halfway through the campaign, I wrote in my journal of our family's persistence in staying connected: "The circle is still strong, still essential, as we navigate this. We are learning to have our own stories within this grander story." We all add to the story individually, but as one unit, as one circle. Our circle is unbreakable and I have learned that protecting what is within that circle is the most important piece of any adaptation and transition.

———— ∞∞∞ ————

After Dad gave his convention speech, my siblings left and headed back to their lives, which meant they were physically separated from us on the campaign trail. But only physically. As far as those around us as we journeyed, the Secret Service officially transitioned and seamlessly replaced the Indiana state troopers who had been protecting us the past four years. It was emotional to say goodbye to the men and women who knew details of our lives, who had watched us grow, and who had protected our parents. Literally overnight, that part of our lives, and those people, were gone. In the days following the convention, we found ourselves asking lots of questions and getting used to "new normals." It was here the campaign trail officially started for the Pences, and even though the circumstances had changed and the cars were definitely bigger, I could still glance at the next seat over and find someone who was figuring it out with me, one turn at a time. This made the adjustment not only more doable—but also fun.

We entered into a new reality, a fresh adventure, and yet the main characters were the same. The beginning of the campaign trail was the start of a new chapter for us, but it was the same story. We were the same people on the same path we had always been heading down, even if we did not know it beforehand.

Since that time, I have looked back at words and thoughts written. I have found comfort and smiled to myself at the knowing presence of God when we least expect it. Looking back on journal entries and speeches has shown me providence time and time again. My personal testimony is one in which the effect of previous words written was monumental for me, but more on that later.

Reading back over Dad's convention speech after he had given it was intriguing to me, as he wrote it before any of us knew what the outcome would be.

"Should I have the awesome privilege to serve as your vice president, I promise to keep faith with that conviction, to pray daily for a wise and discerning heart, for who is able to govern this great people of yours without it? My fellow Americans, I believe we have come to another rendezvous with destiny. And I have faith—faith in the boundless capacity of the American people and faith that God can still heal our land."

As my family set out on its journey, we would need faith and we would need each other. The two converged as well. We needed faith in one another, faith that we could get through this tumultuous time of change, and faith that we would never relent in seeing one another through.

Chapter Ten

Determine Your Heroes

Live simply, love generously, care deeply, speak kindly, leave the
rest to God.

—*Ronald Reagan*

I have fond memories of helping my father craft and edit the
speech he gave at the Ronald Reagan Presidential Library
on September 8, 2016. This speech was one of his favorite
things he got to do on the trail, mainly because President Reagan
is a personal hero of his. He was the reason Dad even became a
Republican, having been a youth coordinator for local Democrats
in Bartholomew County, Indiana, as a young man. We worked on
the speech on the five-hour plane ride to California from Indiana.
Mom couldn't go on this trip, so it was up to me to help out. And I
wanted to go, too. As a kid, we had taken a vacation to California
and visited the Reagan Library at Dad's insistence. He always was,
and still is, eager to share his inspirations with us.

In the latter part of the speech he gave, Dad commented on
President Reagan's impact on his own life. "I like to open the Old
Book every morning," he said. "One of my favorite verses is: 'If you
owe debts pay debts, if honor, then honor, if respect, then respect.'

And more than anything else, I am here today first to pay a debt of honor and a debt of gratitude to someone whose example, whose eloquence, whose broad-shouldered leadership in so many ways has inspired my small life and will continue to inspire any contributions I am able to make to this great country." He told the story about when he had the chance to meet President Reagan the first time he ran for Congress in 1988. Dad would go on to lose that race, but in the course of it he attended a meet-and-greet with the sitting president and other candidates. As he was getting ready for his turn to say hello to Reagan, he was nervous. He felt as if he was supposed to tell Reagan something about the constituents he was hoping to represent or ask for specific funding for the district, but he wanted to say something meaningful he could tell his grandkids about.

He turned to Mom, who was with him, and told her this. She smiled at him and said, "Just say what's on your heart." And he did.

Dad recalled this moment in his speech at the Reagan Library: "I said, 'I just want to thank you. I want to thank you for everything you've done to inspire my generation to believe in this country again.' And for the rest of my life, I'll always believe that in that moment, the fortieth president of the United States...blushed. And he said, 'Well, Mike, that's a very nice thing of you to say.'" At this point, Dad did a Reagan impression that got laughter and applause from the crowd.

Dad also commented on the honor he had to go to Reagan's funeral and quoted Margaret Thatcher's remarks given there. "'We here still move in twilight,' she said, 'but we have one beacon to guide us that Ronald Reagan never had. We have his example.'"

The crowd was enraptured, captivated, and as Dad addressed them, the energy in the room caused me to think back to when President Reagan passed away. Dad made sure to take his kids down to the Capitol, where the president's body would lay in state for a few days. We were living in Arlington, Virginia, at the time. It was the summer after my fourth-grade year and it was especially hot outside. The horse-drawn caisson drove through Washington, D.C., in full ceremonial form and soldiers of every branch lined the streets, frozen in salute. I remember standing on the edge of the street with Dad, watching as the final motorcade drove by. I caught a glimpse of it and right before it went by, a soldier nearby fainted. The members of the military had been standing for hours, unmoving, waiting to pay a final salute to their former commander in chief, and this man would rather faint than move. That dedication and respect moved me as a young child, and still does. It is not lost on me how some may view my own father this way. While I love and respect him, and would defend him against anyone, I cannot fully appreciate or understand this view of him since he will always be my father first. I can never really know the level of respect that exists, not for him as a person, but for the position he holds, the country and the people he represents, and I will always be humble and moved by it.

We waited in line at the service for a while and walked through the rotunda, the room hushed and quiet in remembrance and respect. Americans traveled from all over the country to come and say goodbye. I remember hearing from people—Republicans, Democrats, Independents—who had come from their home states for the specific purpose of showing how much the president's life and work had meant to them. He had a connection with everyday people, and the words he spoke transcended party lines and got through to everyone on all spectrums of the political sphere.

Dad went on in his speech to discuss the policies of Donald Trump and how he would impact America the way Reagan did, if elected president. He remarked on the kind of leader he would be. I have thought a lot about leadership over the past year and have come to a main conclusion about it.

Leadership is lonely.

It separates you from others in a physical, emotional, and mental way. On the campaign trail, I felt this detachment and saw it as an adult rather than as the little kid who had grown up following my parents around, wistfully blind to workplace dynamics. When I was younger, I would run in and out of my parents' social circles, never wondering what was going on within them, never questioning why we never went to staff parties or celebratory dinners. We just went home, because we were a family, we were kids, and that was what we did.

When I was older, though, I realized that leadership comes with some other rules that aren't necessarily spoken. To take the lead on something, you have to seek advice. You have to have followers, but you also have to be out on your own a little bit. To be in the forefront means to be separated and it can be isolating at times. It puts you in front of the pack, so much so that you can't necessarily see the people running along behind you even though you know they are there.

The American Dream means you can accomplish whatever measure of success you desire, rather than what everyone else thinks of as successful. Many of those on the "lower rungs" of a company are perfectly happy to be there, and I get it now. Because leadership is hard.

I was on the leadership team at my camp before the presidential campaign happened in our lives. And on a much different scale I was able to experience how leadership felt, as I was in charge of a staff of counselors. This experience was one I hadn't had before in a professional sense. The people I was in charge of were looking to me for decisions, and I eventually realized they didn't care what my decision was as much as they just wanted someone to make it and tell them what to do. That's what a boss does. Sometimes, employees don't like the choice their boss makes, but that is the role and someone must do it.

You don't have to be in a position of power to identify with this concept. Being someone with values who speaks out in support of them is also something that can be lonely. This doesn't mean we should be afraid of using our voices. Although it can be isolating at times, it is necessary and real.

I find this seems to happen a lot to people in their twenties: They are figuring out how to be on their own while also defining who they want to be in adulthood. Being in your twenties is often spoken of by adults as a wonderful time of freedom and limited responsibility. Yet, the reality for me and for other twentysomethings I know is that this is not the case.

For people in their twenties, it can be a confusing time. We are trying to decide who we want to be, what we want to do, and with whom we want to spend time, and all this while becoming financially independent. It can be an especially isolating time, as we are determining what values we want to hold fast to as adults.

Adults are typically more settled in their careers and have a better idea of the goals they want to accomplish. If you try and do this before you are thirty, like I have, people sometimes think this is strange. They tell you to "just enjoy your twenties," and "have fun," but there you are, feeling stagnant, feeling like you want to make a difference and don't have any idea how. You want to be a leader and become like the people you have grown up admiring, but the path is not as clear while you are on it. But I have come to realize things are never clear in the present moment. The adults I admire went through times of indecision and struggle, too. They felt lonely at times, but they kept their faith in the bigger picture. And that was what made the difference.

Leadership is lonely. It can be isolating to take a stand, but many important things are.

Thinking back to that speech my father gave at the Reagan Library, he shared wisdom that helps me when I'm weary, wondering how to inspire positive change, or when I feel discouraged and isolated, with seasoned ambition but uncertainty about the right method. When Dad looked out at the crowd of Reagan fans and ended his speech, he talked about leadership. One of his lines specifically stood out to me, and it is one I came back to when writing this book: "Honesty is the axis on which leadership spins," he said. Honesty is essential in leading others, but it is also a way in which it can detach the leader from the rest of the group. For one to be an effective leader, decisions must be made and orders must be followed. People are more likely to follow a leader whom they trust. Being honest with one's team is a way to earn that trust, but leadership often requires making decisions with the full scope of knowledge that one's subordinates may not have. This is where honesty in daily life comes into play. If we live our lives with integrity and ambition to make a difference and follow our dreams, we may face challenges alone. The key to navigating this reality is finding people who inspire us and teach us. Leadership is lonely, but when we find others who have gone down the path before, who have carved out the way and left us clues to guide our steps, we find encouragement and refuge in their example.

Chapter Eleven

Take the Time to Remember

The world will little note, nor long remember what we say here, but it can never forget what they did here. It is for us the living, rather, to be dedicated here to the unfinished work which they who fought here have thus far so nobly advanced.

— *President Abraham Lincoln*, Gettysburg Address

The campaign trail is a blur. It's a whirlwind for family, staff, security, and the press. But there were times when Dad took his time, when he knew something was important and his attention was especially needed. Sometimes to the detriment of the schedule, his punctuality, or his staff's patience, he would decide that a certain place or person needed more time than the day's agenda allotted for, and so his decision ruled.

One such place was Gettysburg.

In the press reports of that day, there was a hilarious tidbit that said Dad's right-hand man and longtime assistant had unsuccessfully tried to keep him on schedule. This happened on the bus tour part of the trip, and we were riding through the rolling hills of Pennsylvania. A guide for the battlefield was there, too, and he was detailing the history of each place as we rode on.

Dad and I got out for a scheduled stop to pay our respects at the monument for Hoosiers who had lost their lives. It was sobering as we looked at the hills, now grown over, decades of footprints having crossed, and where so many men had passed away in the heat of battle. I thought about how special a place it truly is, what it says about us as Americans and humans that we dedicate spaces of mass loss to be remembered and taken care of forever.

Dad was a history major as an undergraduate and his love for times past has never left him. He kept asking the guide every question he could think of, not letting up, and I wondered when was the last time the guide had encountered a politician so eager to learn.

The bus bumped along and the guide pointed out the window.

"And this is the hill where Lincoln made his famous address at Gettysburg."

It was the entry to the Soldiers' National Cemetery, blocked off by a gate, and we couldn't quite see the exact location.

Dad peered out the window, then turned back to the guide.

"Well, can we go see it?"

The guide looked to the other staffers huddled on the bus for guidance.

"We can do whatever you'd like, sir."

"Yeah," Dad said without a second thought. "I'd like to go see it."

As detailed in the press pool report of the day, his loyal assistant could be heard from the back calling, "Governor! Governor!" to let him know there wasn't any time for more stops.

Dad waved him off the bus as it came to a stop. "Come on, we're going to go see where he gave the speech."

The assistant shrugged his shoulders and laughed. "I had to try," I heard him say.

I followed Dad off the bus and he waited for me as I caught up to the group. I was reminded of so many car rides and road trips of my childhood when he would make an unscheduled stop because there was something important he didn't want us to miss.

One particular stop happened on our way to summer camp when I was around eleven years old. Every year while Dad worked in Congress, we went to Summer's Best Two Weeks, a Christian summer sports camp on a lake in northern Pennsylvania—and possibly one of the first places where I met Christians who were, to me, really cool.

Each year, it was about a three-hour drive from where we lived in Arlington, Virginia, to the massive lake where the camp was located. Michael and Audrey went most years, too, and Mom and Dad loaded up our minivan with all of our belongings and drove us all up. I was always so nervous on that ride, being somewhat of a homebody and knowing I was going to get homesick the moment I was dropped off and my parents drove away. On this particular year, Dad had already decided on making an extra stop when we got close to the camp.

We turned off the highway and the country roads we saw meant that we were almost there. Dad took a different turn, though, and we noticed we were headed in the opposite direction of the camp. After a few minutes, it was clear his course was intentional and from the backseat of the minivan we asked where we were going. He told us we were twenty minutes from where Flight 93 had gone down on September 11, and he wanted to see the site for himself, having never visited it.

He drove up to a small parking lot at the end of one of the country roads and we all got out to see. The site wasn't marked with a memorial yet. There was no visitor center and no way to come and plant a tree. All these things would be added in time, but back then it was just a plaque on the side of the road, a flag, and a field.

Dad read the inscription on the plaque and pointed to show Michael where the plane had gone down.

I looked out toward the field where everyday citizens had become heroes in an instant.

Dad put his arm on my shoulder and said, "These people saved your dad's life."

I nodded; I knew. That plane had presumably been headed for the Capitol, and since he was in Congress at the time, he would have been there. A lot of people lost their dads on that day, but I didn't, and I had these souls to be forever indebted to.

⚬⚬⚬

Back at Gettysburg, we hiked up into a field to look through the fence where President Lincoln had given the famous Gettysburg Address on November 19, 1863. It turned out to be a much longer walk than anticipated, and when the guide told Dad this, he of course waved it off as we knew he would. He really wanted to see it.

When we finally arrived at the area, the guide pointed to show us where the site of Lincoln's speech was, just a small hill, a mound where people would have been able to see the president speak, but nothing grand.

Lincoln had delivered the address at a dedication of the Soldiers' National Cemetery and as the story goes, he actually finished writing it that day before the ceremony began. It reminds me of someone else I know who scribbles last-minute phrases on note card speeches before delivering them.

Dad crossed his arms and looked through the fence, considering it and taking in the scene.

"I've never been here," he told the guide. "I've come to Gettysburg and I have never seen where he gave the speech."

Charlotte and Mike Pence share a family moment. *(Karen Pence)*

Charlotte and her mom embrace on a joyful Christmas morning. *(Mike Pence)*

The three Pence children, Audrey, Michael, and Charlotte *(l to r)*, with their dad. *(Karen Pence)*

Mike Pence teaches Charlotte how to ride a horse. *(Karen Pence)*

The Pence family takes a western vacation and enjoys the scenery. *(Karen Pence)*

Charlotte and her dad spend some time at a horse barn. *(Karen Pence)*

The Pence family takes a horse trail ride on vacation. *(Mike Pence)*

The Pence family vacations together on a beach in Sanibel, Florida. *(Nancy Fritsch)*

Charlotte Pence spends time at the beach in 1998. *(Karen Pence)*

The Pence kids support their dad at his radio show on the weekend of the Indy 500. *(Karen Pence)*

The Pence family visits the U.S. Capitol during the holidays. *(Karen Pence)*

The Pence family at Pet Night, an annual event on Capitol Hill. *(Animal Health Institute)*

The Pence family meets Frank the Pug from *Men in Black* while attending Pet Night. *(Karen Pence)*

Charlotte meets First Lady Laura Bush at the annual White House Picnic. *(Mike Pence)*

The Pence children attend Memorial Day ceremonies at Arlington Cemetery and wave to President Bush's motorcade. *(Karen Pence)*

Vice President and Second Lady Pence smile for the camera in front of the land where Charlotte's great-grandfather grew up in Ireland. *(Charlotte Pence)*

Charlotte relaxes with her dad at the Aynes House in southern Indiana, where the Pence family spent many of their weekends during her father's term as governor of Indiana. *(Karen Pence)*

The Pence family spends time together backstage after Mike Pence's speech accepting the Republican nomination for vice president at the 2016 Republican National Convention. *(Annie Poynter)*

Mike and Karen Pence take a photo with the Pence family dog, Maverick, for National Dog Day. (*Zach Bauer*)

Charlotte attends the 2017 March for Life with her parents in Washington, D.C. (*Marc Lotter*)

The Pences put pins in this map of the United States whenever they visited a city on the campaign trail. (*Amelia Cassar*)

Mike Pence gives a speech at a rally in the pouring rain.
(McKenzie Barbknecht)

The Pences visit the North Carolina GOP headquarters that was bombed during the 2016 campaign. (*Amelia Cassar*)

A couch from inside the North Carolina GOP headquarters that was damaged in the attack. (*Amelia Cassar*)

Charlotte votes on Election Day 2016 in Indianapolis, Indiana. *(Vaughn Hillyard)*

Charlotte hugs her dad as the election results start to come in. *(Karen Pence)*

Vice President Mike Pence takes a selfie with his family as they wait for results to come in on election night. *(Mike Pence)*

The Pence family huddles for a quick prayer as the results of the election start to be called. *(Nick Ayers)*

The Pence family's relatives in Doonbeg, Ireland, hang a celebratory sign on the door of their family-owned pub the day after the 2016 election. *(Hugh McNally)*

Charlotte dances with her father at a family wedding. (*Todd Parker*)

Charlotte spends quality time with her dad on a summer day in Indiana. (*Karen Pence*)

He took a moment, asked me if I was ready, and we headed back to the bus.

As we walked, I thought about this field where such a deadly and consequential battle had taken place. I thought of the families who never got to have their loved ones come home to them from war, who never got to say a proper goodbye.

Just like that other field in Pennsylvania I had visited as a child, and my parents would visit yet again on Dad's first September 11 as vice president, everyday Americans became heroes here. They fought for liberty, for ideals, for their country, and it is up to us to carry on that fight.

As survivors, sometimes it seems as though we can do so little other than to simply do our best to remember. As Lincoln said in his address, "But, in a larger sense, we cannot dedicate—we cannot consecrate—we cannot hallow—this ground. The brave men, living and dead, who struggled here, have consecrated it, far above our poor power to add or detract."

When traveling with Mom and Dad to Europe after the election, we went to the Dachau Concentration Camp. I had never been to one of the camps before. It was difficult, impactful, and sickening. To view a place such as Dachau, now arranged as a sort of museum, and to know of the horrors that took place there, brings with it a range of emotions.

The most moving part of the visit was the person who took us through the camp. He was a Holocaust survivor and had actually been at Dachau. He'd lost his family members in the camps and to look at him was to see someone who has experienced a degree of loss and suffering I cannot fathom but from whose life I must try to learn.

Leaving Dachau that day, I considered the purpose of going to such a place. We have to visit these places and remind ourselves of the horrors committed there so as to never allow them to happen again. We also have to do this in order to recognize the evils of the times we live in and do whatever is in our power to stop them from happening.

But I couldn't shake the question I asked myself: *Is it enough?*

The answer I came up with is: *No.* Of course it isn't enough, but it is something, and if everyone does something, then we change the world.

I cannot add to history; I cannot detract from the acts of those heroes on Flight 93, or of soldiers who have lost their lives in battle, or of this survivor of genocide.

Lincoln must have felt a similar burden of inability when he spoke to those soldiers over a century and a half ago. We know there were unplanned additions to this famous speech, "unscheduled stops," if you will, and oftentimes in my experience those tend to be the most valuable. I hold fast to the final paragraph, his advice to the ages that have lived on and inspired people all over the world for decades. Perhaps this was a spontaneous addition, perhaps not. History can only know.

Chapter Twelve

Don't Be Afraid to Be the D.C. Hillbillies

*Thank you, God, for the little moments of fun and laughter that
    we have.*
May we always notice them.

—My Campaign Trail Journal, July 2016

For me the hardest day of the campaign trail was October 20, 2016.

We had a long week in front of us and took an early morning flight out to Las Vegas, ready for a full day's work, which would mean four plane rides to four different states. We had started the day in Indianapolis and had flown west to begin the trek. I spent the ride as I usually did, working through a book I was reading or taking notes on scripts for the production company I consulted for. Traveling over the mountains to the desert plains, I may have slept a bit or turned around in my seat to chat with Mom and Dad about the upcoming agenda. I had gotten Dad the first book in the Harry Potter series to read on the trail, and he was just starting it, enjoying it a lot. We might have talked about that. I don't remember the exact specifics of that trip, but as so often is the case when an event enters our lives and upends it, I remember everything that follows.

We landed in Vegas, our phones came back on, and Mom leaned forward in her seat and reached through to where I sat. Her hand tugged on my shoulder and I heard strained urgency in her voice.

"Charlotte, Charlotte, guys," she said, leaning over to Dad to get his attention.

I peeked through the space in between the chairs and saw her holding Dad's hand. She reached through the space to grab mine before she spoke, and I knew what it was about.

"Poppa just emailed me. Maverick passed away last night," she whispered. Her voice caught on the last words and I felt her hand squeeze mine. I slumped in my chair, her words settling in. She started to cry and Dad hugged her while I turned back around in my seat.

The tears came just as the press corps was coming off the plane.

Mom was crying, I was crying, and I just couldn't stop. We knew this was coming; we had been prepared for a while now. I am not a particularly emotional person, but with the loss of my childhood dog, as old as he was, I was a mess. The reality of it sunk in and although he had been staying comfortably with my grandpa while we traveled, I couldn't help but think I had abandoned him.

The press saw us and respectfully kept their distance as they exited the plane.

We got into the cars and made our way to the venue for Dad's first speech of many that day. He held it together and as we drove, I had that laugh-cry thing going on as we talked about how bad of a dog Maverick really was.

Dad said, "He wasn't a bad dog. He was just bad at being a dog," and I could have sworn the Secret Service agents in the front seat chuckled to themselves.

Maverick witnessed many a Pence family memory and he had campaigned with us all over Indiana, too. He was really my brother's dog. We had surprised him with a beagle when he was away at Boy Scouts camp in the fifth grade. He came back early, though, and found his new puppy in the basement while we were gone.

Maverick came with his name, and so we kept it, feeling as though it fit. He was a rescue, and so had a hard time around grown men, who seemed to frighten him. He was a loving and caring dog who, despite his erratic beagle tendencies, genuinely wanted to please even though his nature was to run away, tear comforters apart, and eat anything in sight.

<hr />

Being on the trail when Maverick passed brought up memories of other pets and how they've been so important, even in the midst of our busy political lives. Maverick wasn't around yet, but one of the most unforgettable things involving our pets took place when we moved out to Washington, D.C., when Dad was elected to Congress the first time. This is a tale of Bud and friends. Bud was a girl and she was named for Dad's favorite beer. Yes, really.

Mom gave Bud to Dad as a surprise Christmas gift one year, and she was their baby before we came along—a gorgeous black Lab mix with curly hair.

As I mentioned, most congressional families don't move to Washington, D.C., opting rather to stay in their home state while the congressperson travels back and forth for votes and constituent meetings. When they visit D.C., there are often themed events that are a nice way for them to meet other families who are in the same situation.

It was through these events that I met many families I ended up babysitting for later on in life, and we made friends with other

kids whose dads were in the House or Senate, since we could relate
to one another on a special level.

One of these gatherings would go down in Pence family history
as a legend of epic proportions, not only because of its ludicrous-
ness, but because it accurately sums up our family's arrival to the
Washington, D.C., area in a neat parable.

The name of the event was Pet Night. It was to take place in
one of the office buildings near the Capitol, a fun space for families to gather for a program where their moms or dads in Congress
could come in between votes.

If you are thinking to yourself that "Pet Night" means "Bring
Your Pet to Capitol Hill Night," I will do you a favor and let you
know that is not, in fact, what it means. Instead, it is a night where
famous pets come by to meet the kids of congressional members—
think the cat from *Stuart Little* or the dog from *Men in Black*.

Normally, this would not be a major misunderstanding, since
even if, perhaps upon first reading of Pet Night, you think it means
Bring Your Pet to Capitol Hill Night, you (and possibly many others) would leave your pets at home, just in case, since this setting
perhaps does not strike one as the perfect location to tote your
furry family members.

Alas, Karen Pence did not think this way.

To a Hoosier, a mom, a carefree lady who wanted her kids
to join the fun of all the *other* congressional kids who would, of
course, be bringing *their* pets to Pet Night, assumedly, pets would
be welcome.

Thus, we loaded Bud, our two cats, Madeleine and Pickle, and
yes, you guessed it (or you probably didn't, actually), a lizard by the
name of Gollum in the minivan and drove to the Hill. No sooner
did we park on the side of the busy D.C. street than Bud took off
running into traffic, pulling Mom on the other end of the leash as
she tried to restrain the dog. I held tight to my orange-and-white

cat, Pickle, whom we had rescued only a few months prior, as we headed up the stone steps to the offices. Audrey had Madeleine in her grip and Michael helped get Bud, while holding a shoebox containing his lizard balanced precariously under one arm.

We met Dad inside the reception in between votes being called. The clocks in the Capitol and the surrounding buildings are designed to let members know when they need to head to the chambers for a vote. They have lights all around the edges, next to the numbers, that light up to give them this information. Like a Cinderella situation, as the clock strikes midnight, they turn back into congressmen and congresswomen. In between the soundings of the clock, though, they were parents, and they were moseying in and out of the room with kids and spouses in tow.

We did our rounds, saying hello to people we knew, and of course, getting our pictures with the famous pets there. I don't know when exactly our mother found out that we had misjudged Pet Night, but it was most likely at some point after Bud tried to run away and before Madeleine threw up a hairball next to Dad's foot as he discussed legislation with another freshman congressman.

At the end of it all, we held our heads high as we left that night and remembered just where our place was in this crazy new life. We were the new kids, and as we lovingly referred to ourselves from that moment on, "the D.C. Hillbillies."

A framed picture of Pet Night hung in the governor's residence all four years we lived there, my brother holding a shoebox with the lizard inside, Audrey and I clinging to our cats, and a leash drifting out of the frame to which good ol' Bud was attached.

The thing to note in the picture are our faces: We are beaming. Our smiles couldn't be bigger, and as I've grown up, I know this isn't because of the three kids. Of course, we would have had fun with that faux pas, having realized the mistake we had made. But we are all laughing because my parents are laughing, because they learned then and there—and would be reminded time and time again—that if you take yourselves too seriously in D.C., you miss all the fun.

———⁂———

Back on the campaign trail, we got to the building where the rally was going to take place, and as we walked in, I could hear the crowd cheering as the announcer introduced Dad onstage. I made a quick turn into the greenroom and sat down at one of the tables. Normally, I sat out front with Mom or hung around behind the curtain, taking notes on the speech. This time I couldn't face it. Something had been knocked out of me and I needed a minute.

One of our staffers came in and smiled kindly at me. I just sobbed quietly in the chair.

"You know," he said, "we lost our dog last year. After, I just kept reminding myself how now she can run free and she is enjoying herself, you know?"

I nodded and wiped my nose. Of course he was right. Maverick was old and his health had been failing, but he was "home" to me and now he was gone.

Up to that point, no matter where the campaign had taken us, we were still going home. At the end of the day, the week, the four- or five-state run, we were going back to Indiana, and we were going back to Maverick. Now he wouldn't be there when we returned and there was something empty and final about that.

I was forced to accept the fact that home was changing. It was never going to be exactly the same as it was, and I couldn't hold on to it anymore. I couldn't delude myself into thinking that nothing would change, that after this limbo we were in, everything would go back to normal. It wouldn't. We were leaving home. Win or lose, home would never be the same as it was.

The funny thing about pets is, while they may get you into hilarious situations, they always end up teaching you a lesson at the same time. A part of me knows Maverick was doing just that in choosing his timing to leave this world. He was letting me know that while I had to give him away for now, the memories we had shared, much like those of my home, my childhood, and my family before this 2016 adventure, would still remain.

True, home was changing for my family yet again. But if I had learned anything from living the life of a political child, it was that home is not a physical place. Home is our people, our memories, and the steps we take together into the unknown. When Maverick died, Dad sent pictures of him around to all of us, reminding us of who he was and the rambunctious, hilarious addition he had been to our family. This helped me to focus on the good and appreciate all the special moments we had shared.

In his passing, Maverick taught me a lesson about faith and reminded me of a characteristic I so admire about my parents. They taught me to be fluid and open, to accept change as it comes and trust God with the outcome. But they also showed me to proudly hang those pictures of my failures, to laugh at the silly mistakes, and to run eagerly toward the next adventure without forgetting the past.

Chapter Thirteen

Find Your Group of Happy Warriors

You have not chosen one another, but I have chosen you for one another.

—C. S. Lewis, The Four Loves

Mom said we needed a map—a big one, the whole country, all fifty states, and colorful. We needed pushpins we could stick into every city we'd been to. We tried to make them color coordinated at first, but that fell apart quickly as we visited up to four cities a day and ended up using any and every pin we could find.

We hung it front and center on the plane—the very first thing you would see as you arrived if you were taking a trip with us. It was probably Mom's twenty-plus years of teaching elementary kids that instigated the acquiring of the map in the first place, but I think she also knew we would need reminding of the places we had been with empty spots serving as an ever-changing landscape of possibility.

On one rainy October night, we were scheduled to land at LaGuardia Airport in New York. Our group had already been delayed due to weather and spent the afternoon playing football on the grass beside the tarmac in Iowa while we waited for the hold to be lifted.

The flight was smooth enough, but as we got closer to the airport, we noticed some more turbulence than usual and the flight crew told us to expect a bumpy landing. As we neared the runway, it felt like we were going fast and when we touched down, it still felt like we were going fast. I glanced toward a staff member next to me, and we exchanged questioning looks as we felt the plane swerve to the right. Mud splattered up on the windows as we kept bumping along and eventually lurched to a stop.

Glancing around, I saw everyone was a bit rattled. The flight attendants responded perfectly and I looked over my shoulder at my parents and noticed two Secret Service agents already out of their seats, next to Mom and Dad, emergency kits in hand.

Someone behind me said, "We're off the runway."

Dad asked if Mom and I were okay. I nodded, and then he was up and checking on those around us. I saw his back as he made his way to the rear of the plane to check on the members of our press pool. He would later tell me he didn't think twice about it. "I thought of their parents," he said. "If it were you back there, I'd want someone in authority to be checking on you."

We couldn't see clearly out the windows, but I noticed red lights flashing almost immediately and emergency vehicles arrived within seconds.

Everyone was fine, but we needed to evacuate the plane, and since there were members of the press traveling with us, we knew it would be a story, too. People started calling their family members to let them know they were okay, and my parents called my brother and sister. Michael, who I mentioned is a pilot in the Marine Corps, told our dad to go thank the pilots. "They probably just saved your life," he said, and he was right. We later learned that the pilots' intuition to turn off the runway, into the breakable side of the tarmac, allowed for the plane to stop without heading straight into the New York City highway.

The next day, we were back on the trail, on a new plane, heading out to North Carolina and Pennsylvania. It didn't take long for us to remember: the map. It was still on the other aircraft and since there would be many tests on it for routine investigations into the incident, we wouldn't be seeing that plane again.

The whereabouts of the map remained a mystery for a while. We got it back eventually, but the pins were gone, having been removed or lost. The memory of it remains, though, and that's the most important thing.

Some may say that map was why Trump won. Not the physical piece of it, but the theory behind it. The Trump campaign looked at the empty spots that needed attention, needed pushpins in them. They sent us to the places nobody was going and we listened to the people who felt their opinions hadn't been heard in a long time—the people Donald Trump called "the forgotten men and women" of the forgotten places in America.

I don't know about all that, but I do know we can learn from the lesson the map taught us. I can improve my own life by asking these questions more often. Where are the pushpins in my map? Where are the empty spaces that need tending? Have I been neglecting any spot in particular lately, whether it be health, relationships, writing, or reading?

Maps can be daunting when looked at as a whole, but if we narrow in on the spots we can be present, one step at a time, we end up on an irreplaceable journey that is specific to us as individuals and no one else. Nobody can forge the path for you. No one can visit the areas that only you know need attention. You have to do it on your own, and once you do, you'll look up from that map, from the ground in front of you, and be able to look back at the person you were when you started and see how far you have come.

Mom and Dad took to calling our group of travelers on the campaign trail "Happy Warriors." We went forward in faith and banded together over the course of a few months. There were bumps in the road and a few scary moments, much like the night we landed in New York. No matter what happened, though, we were in it together and we were making the best of the map set before us.

The campaign trail was an unknown landscape all on its own. We knew better than anyone how detrimental and dangerous a misstep might be, but had we not set out on the journey and said yes to the adventure, we would have never known how life-changing our interactions with people along the way would be.

Chapter Fourteen

Debate (and Listen)

We must speak our minds openly, debate our disagreements honestly, but always pursue solidarity.
—President Trump's Inaugural Address, *January 20, 2017*

Growing up, our dinner table was open debating ground. Every night, we'd each talk about our day, and Dad's day happened to include making major policy decisions. In my family, this was the perfect opportunity to jump into action, share our opinions, and challenge one another's opposing views.

For introverted me, though, it could be uncomfortable.

I remember sometimes cringing in my seat, eating chicken and green beans quietly, wondering why we couldn't just talk about the weather, or movies, or something easy. I was wrong, though. We have to talk to each other, debate each other, and learn how to do so without arguing or becoming angry. I learned this at a young age without even realizing it. We were taught to plunge into the unknown, where it was sticky and uncomfortable. My parents showed us how to ask questions and listen instead of tuning out an opinion we didn't like.

Some of my favorite memories from the campaign trail are of debates and debate preps.

I took note of the following after the campaign:

Things that make campaign debates fun:

1. Being a former participant of a debate team in high school (such as Student Congress).
2. Having an amazing dad who lets you help him craft his language and argument.
3. Getting to spontaneously ask said dad questions in the middle of everyday events to keep him on his toes.
4. Being part of a bigger story.

Dad did three practice debates before the vice presidential debate. These were complete with a pretend moderator and someone playing the role of Tim Kaine. It was leaked that Dad's friend Governor Scott Walker of Wisconsin played Kaine for the practice, and this is true. Governor Walker was great and they had fun debating points as he tested Dad on potential questions and speech topics.

While practicing at the mock debate venues, whenever he answered a question and wasn't sure how he did, Dad would look over to me, sitting front row among the small audience of staffers who had gathered, and I would look up from the notes I was taking and shoot him a thumbs-up.

And one night sitting in the kitchen, we talked about how he would answer questions regarding women's issues. As always, Dad was intent on hearing my perspective and we worked hard to get his language and tone just right. As Dad and I were going over his answers with a top political aide, he answered the question regarding reproductive rights, and looked to me afterward to ask how he had done. I said he should speak more from the heart, tell a story about why he believes what he does rather than shooting off policy points and data.

Eventually, we got him to a point when his answer was similar to that which he gave in the debate. When it came to this subject, Dad couldn't discuss it without bringing up his faith. However, there was a way to do this without excluding others who don't share the same religious beliefs as him. In the debate, Dad commented, "For me, the sanctity of human life proceeds out of the belief—that ancient principle—where God says, 'Before you were formed in the womb, I knew you.'" He went on to add how Indiana is on its way to becoming the most pro-adoption state. "I think if you're going to be pro-life, you should be pro-adoption... Like Mother Theresa said at that famous national prayer breakfast, 'Let's welcome the children into our world.'" Dad wrapped up his point with compassion. "A society can be judged by how it deals with its most vulnerable: the aged, the infirm, the disabled, and the unborn. I believe it with all my heart."

Before Dad took the stage on the night of the debate, he spent time praying with Mom and we all gave him a hug before we took our seats. I may never know exactly how he felt in that moment, but it must have been similar to having the weight of the world's expectations on your shoulders and hoping you had done enough to answer correctly. That is when faith takes over.

We watched from the front row, on the edges of our seats. I was fairly animated at the end of the row next to Mom, throwing my hands up occasionally when I grew frustrated. My siblings teased me about this later, but I had been to a few other debates and knew it was all right as long as I didn't create too much of a commotion.

Afterward, we went up onstage to congratulate Dad and shake Senator Kaine's hand. Audrey called Dad from abroad, where she was working in Tanzania, and he answered on live television. The media did their best to find out who had called him, speculating that it was perhaps Trump. When CNN zoomed in to the phone to see the caller ID, it read, "The Best Daughter in the World" and that was the end of that story.

In the moments after, Dad told us he thought it was a draw— and I think he still does. He said Kaine did a great job and he thought it was pretty equal. Backstage, and into the next few weeks, people said Dad won the debate, but maybe the reason he didn't see it this way is simply because he respects the theory of debates, as do I, as does my family.

Winners of debates are primarily decided based on who was able to argue their point most effectively, since in reality, no one can really win at something entirely opinion-based and biased. A liberal audience may have deemed Tim Kaine the winner, a conservative audience siding more with Dad, but I think the mere act of declaring a winner is counterproductive.

Maybe we shouldn't view debates as places where we can either win or lose. That might ultimately lead to not debating at all for fear of losing, or only discussing topics with people whom we know we agree. There are experts who can decide in an unbiased manner the winner of debates, but does that notion simply lead us to a combative culture of winning and losing, of cheering as if we are rooting for a specific sports team? If so, should we be okay with this act of declaring winners and losers?

I'm grateful I can always go back to the Pence family dinner table, where debate winners and losers were maybe known but never named. Conversations led to disagreements, but never without reconciliation, understanding, and an ultimate acceptance that while we may never convince someone to agree on our points, we can absolutely try to see from their perspective and they to see from ours.

Chapter Fifteen

Be the Reminder

To think how little we actually know about the big picture at any given moment can be something so terrifying, yet when it really comes down to it, it is really invigorating.

—My Campaign Trail Journal, December 2016

D uring the campaign, there were terrible storms in Louisiana, and massive amounts of flooding had destroyed entire communities. We took a trip down there with Donald Trump after people had been able to get back into their homes and emergency personnel gave us the all clear to come in.

Entire homes had been cleared out. We drove down streets and saw people dragging all of their belongings out onto their driveways—couches, tables, beds, stacked high awaiting removal. Everything inside the flooded homes had been ruined.

We brought supplies and loaded trucks at a shelter before heading to a neighborhood to visit a family that had lost everything. We walked into the empty home that had been gutted and saw the lines on the walls where the water had risen. The man who owned the home told us how he had been born in the small house next door and built this house on his own. He had lived there his entire life, raised his family there, and had hoped to live there for the rest of his days. Now he wasn't sure. They had already rebuilt the structure once and he told us he wasn't sure if he had it in him to do it again.

Dad patted him on the back and we gave his wife a hug as she stood beside him, nodding in solemn agreement.

Donald Trump did something different, though. He looked around and surveyed the home, most likely drawing on his expertise in real estate and construction. He nodded confidently, looked right at the man, and said, "You're going to rebuild. I can tell you're that kind of person. You're going to rebuild."

The man lit up, his eyes locked on the person who would one day be his president. He nodded and continued to show us the exterior area of the house. Something in his demeanor had changed, though, and I have thought back to it many times. He had confidence and pride in this place, and it showed as he pointed out the improvements he had made to the house over time.

It was almost a year later that we heard from that family again. The man had, in fact, built a new home. Trump's confidence in him was possibly exactly what he needed. He didn't need us to come see his house and pity his situation. Rather, he needed someone to see through the situation to the future—to have faith in him to not give up on his dream. Life had thrown him into an unexpected spot, as it so often does. Sometimes we just need someone who is going to look us in the eye, realize our potential, and not let us forget it.

Sometimes unexpected things happen that can knock us down and take the breath out of us, knock the wind out of our sails. We can allow this to keep us down for a while, and then we can pick ourselves back up and face the new situation head-on. It isn't always that easy, though. Sometimes we need other people to help us out and look us straight in the eyes, tell us they believe in us and they know we are going to do just fine.

I have had moments in my life like this, too, when I needed a person to believe in me, to tell me I had support no matter what happened. Specifically, I think back to when I was a freshman in college. I was having a hard time adjusting and finding what it was I wanted to do with my life. I knew I wanted to work in filmmaking, but I had so many interests in other areas of my life as well. It was right before spring break and I was planning to go on a trip instead of come home for the week. I called my parents to ask their advice about what I should do in regards to majoring in something different—or double-majoring or minoring. I felt pressure to figure out what to do and not waste my time. I didn't know then that I would go on to study abroad at the University of Oxford or that I would double-major in English so I could focus on creative writing. All I knew was that I felt stressed and the way before me was foggy and clouded.

I called Mom and she put Dad on the phone. He was dealing with an important issue at the time—I don't remember what it was. But he stopped everything. He listened. He heard the fear and anxiety in my voice and when I was finished talking, he simply said, "You're coming home for spring break. We're going to figure this out. You're not trapped. You're coming home."

And I did. And we had many "Dad talks," as I would go on to fondly name them. We had many of those throughout college and they continue to this day. Whenever I feel overwhelmed and my thoughts are crowded, I know I can go to him and he can help me clear them up.

We need people in our lives to remind us to listen.

It is easy to get confused and lost. We can hear the pressures of the world instead of the peace we know to exist. I don't mean to make the case that this is an easy thing to do. That's why we need other people in our lives to do it for us.

I told Dad he would be good at this job. Mom told me I would be okay with the decision I needed to make. And much later on in our lives, when things had changed drastically in our family, candidate Trump told the man in Louisiana he would rebuild.

We need these reminders at all times—whether it be in the calm or the storm. For the storms will come, and it will be the steady strength of our loved ones in the peaceful times that we will lean on in the uncertainty.

Chapter Sixteen

Don't Let the Little Things Become the Big Things

If you can keep your head when all about you
Are losing theirs and blaming it on you,
If you can trust yourself when all men doubt you,
But make allowance for their doubting too . . .

　　　　　　　　　　　　—Rudyard Kipling, "If"

Halloween of 2016 was the spookiest I have ever experienced. Perhaps it was our imagination, tension, or stress getting the best of us, but if you are inclined to have any belief in the supernatural, as I am, perhaps you will see something different. The election was a week away, and "tired" doesn't even begin to describe how everyone was feeling, but the flight crew was fantastic. My two favorite flight attendants had decorated the entire cabin of the plane with Halloween decorations and we had special treats on our trip to the first rally of the day.

On the night of October 31, 2016, we had a typical day—a long one with a few rallies in different cities. The final event was in an airport hangar. These were my favorite, as we would fly in, land on the runway, and taxi over to the hangar, where hundreds of people would be waiting for us. They cheered, waving signs and flags with media set up behind them. It was typical of Dad to exit the plane and literally run to the crowd, taking the stage with a smile like a little kid and two thumbs up.

This night was no different except for the families with kids dressed in Halloween costumes. It was dark outside, but the hangar was brightly lit and Dad began his speech as Mom and I took our seats to the right of the stage.

Anyone who has worked closely with Dad knows him to be a physical note-taker. By this, I mean he writes his speeches out on note cards in his own handwriting, scribbles edits on them, and then uses these when he speaks to hundreds, if not thousands, of people. These note cards during the campaign were a legend in themselves, as they had endured as many states, cities, climates, plane rides, hotel rooms, early mornings, and late nights as we had.

At one of our outdoor events in Virginia, he got out of the car, ready to take the stage, when a torrential downpour started. A few people wondered if we should cancel the event—especially since umbrellas are not allowed in the crowd for security reasons. Dad looked at Mom and in one glance they both decided there would be no canceling—these people had waited long enough to hear his message and if they wanted to stay, then so would he. He took the stage, sans umbrella just like the crowd, and spoke. By the end, everyone's clothes were completely soaked through, including Dad's, but the amazing thing was nobody left. Back on the plane— "Trump Force Two," as we had nicknamed it—the stewards prepared hot drinks and extra blankets for everyone. The note cards were not spared from the storm and the staff helped lay them out carefully to dry on tray tables and seats. They dried off eventually and Dad continued to use them—wrinkled and slightly blurred.

On Halloween, he pulled these same note cards out of his suit pocket and began, but strange things started to happen. About half-way through his speech, the lights went out and we could no longer hear him speaking. There were safety lights in the facility, but he wasn't lit on the stage and Mom and I signaled to him that his microphone was out, too. A member of our advance team jogged to the front, carrying a bullhorn, and true to the show-must-go-on mind-set of our group, Dad turned it on, took the stage, and the crowd cheered. Members of our team found some heavy-duty flashlights and shined them on him as he continued.

When he was done, he worked the rope line as usual and Mom brought him a bucket of candy for them both to pass out to the kids on the line who were decked out in costumes. I met one girl in particular who was wearing a long yellow dress and informed me she was Ivanka Trump for Halloween. I snapped a picture of us and told her I would tell Ivanka.

As we finished the rope line, Dad signed a few signs and posters for the facility and did a quick local television interview, and we all made our way back to the plane. It wasn't long before we realized something was missing: the note cards.

A few people hurried back to the podium where Dad had left them, but they were gone. We searched the area, asked the workers at the facility, but nobody could find them. Time was running out, as the crew needed to take off within a certain window due to their flight plan. We did the best we could, but in the confusion of the rally, the note cards went missing and we had to leave without them.

Everyone was disappointed. It felt like we had lost a friend, a companion, a fellow staffer who had been through the thick of it and come out on the other side with us. Those note cards told a story—the story of resilience, the essence of the Trump–Pence campaign, and they had successfully carried the message all over the country.

As we flew over a sleeping America that night, we all felt the sadness of this settling in and Dad felt it, too. We each thought it was our own fault for not checking and double-checking that we had them. We said we would look at the security tapes, find the person who took them, whether it was intentional or not, and get them back, but it has been almost a year since those note cards went missing and they still have not been found.

Dad was quiet for a while. Then he pulled out some blank note cards and began writing on them. He had basically memorized the speech at this point and although those cards were sentimental to us, they could be replaced. They were only objects, items, things, that we had put our faith in over time to get us from event to event. The importance we had put on them, at the end of the day, was really artificial. He could give the speech on his own; he could rewrite the notes and everything would still go smoothly.

I remember turning around in my seat as I often did to talk to my parents when I was bored on the flights. I flipped around with my knees at the back of the chair and leaned over the top. He looked up at me and I nodded toward the staff. He smiled and turned to them.

"It's okay," he said to them. "It's okay."

A few of our veteran team members still had their heads hung in shame. When something goes wrong with a group this close, everybody feels the weight of the responsibility.

Dad called out to a few in particular until they looked at him and made eye contact.

"It's okay," he said again, until finally they nodded and accepted his forgiveness.

That night, back at the hotel, one member of the staff said to me, "I just never want to let him down." It is this spirit of our group I was inspired by time and time again—their dedication and loyalty to my parents and to the team, their fierce determination in having our back no matter what happened. But things do happen. Mistakes are made, and the true test of a team, the true test of a leader, is how we respond in those situations.

It wasn't the perfect, unflawed, seamless events with no hiccups and clean, dry note cards that would prove our resilience. It was the lack of such—and whatever filled in the gaps. Little things can become the big things if we let them, if we choose to focus on those problems instead of remembering the bigger picture.

In the absence of the note cards, we had forgiveness, grace, and the clarity of our message. We remembered why we were on the journey, the people we were intent on helping and representing, and the path that had led us there.

Perhaps the note cards were becoming a crutch, allowing us to be complacent and stop rethinking the job and how to do it best. Oftentimes in life, we continue to go through the motions, read from a script of the life we have made for ourselves instead of looking up and out at the people who got us to where we are, who are cheering us on in our daily accomplishments and setbacks.

Perhaps sometimes we need to lose the note cards to know we never needed them at all.

Chapter Seventeen

Honor Your Mom

When I need to be reminded of who I am and what my tendencies are, it always helps to look to my parents—specifically, my wonderful mother.

—My Campaign Trail Journal, July 2016

The real heroes of a story are often not the protagonists. They are the people who are least noticed, who encourage the main character with their very presence. They stand to the sidelines, watching, cheering, and uplifting. They pick up the pieces and glue the warrior back together before pushing him into the arena. In this story, the unspoken champion is always and forever my mom.

I don't know how people get through life without a mom like mine. I genuinely wonder about this and have a lot of respect for people who can navigate this crazy world without a Karen Pence to turn to. It must take immeasurable skill. Mom and I often joke we are the same person. It's true we have numerous similarities in our personalities, and I can only hope to be as strong as she is one day. Most people do not know very much about their Second Lady. This is to be expected, as the spouses of political figures tend to get less attention. People mainly assume they are doing the duties expected of them and tend to forget about them. Less interest is shown in their *real* job, on which I wish to shed some light.

I have grown up to understand the political spouses are the real champions. They take criticism and insults positioned to hurt them, but more than that, they have to watch as their partner in life deals with the pressures and inevitable difficulties that come with public service. All while doing this, they often have families to look out for as well, and they take on this heavy burden with grace and deliberation. They are not only active participants in the public service role of their spouses, even though they are not technically elected, but they also climb the mountain of publicity in their personal life, step by step, guiding their children along the way. It is their job to hold up their spouse when the public servant cannot continue on his or her own, and to protect them when their schedules become too much to handle and they risk getting too run-down.

The few months we spent together on the trail created a sce-nario in which my parents and I were roommates, navigating a political culture of which we had been a small part in the past, but never to this extent. I acted as their manager, assistant, coach, personal trainer, dietician, friend, confidante, and daughter, all at the same time.

It was the greatest experience of my life thus far and as I watched Dad navigate his role, I couldn't miss Mom there, too. She was everywhere he was, right by his side, and on days when she had to stay home in Indiana to take care of family things, he missed her.

Since she didn't have an official assistant traveling with her, I played this part, helping her figure out her schedule, manage phone calls, and prepare for media interviews. At times, I was the liaison between her and members of the staff or, eventually, the transition team, and I was a part of most, if not all, her meetings.

We had a great time, it was fun, but along the way, she also taught me about leadership through her example. I had the incredible experience of having my mom also be my boss, which is not something most people get.

I watched from the sidelines and took notes on Dad and his speeches, but I was taking mental notes about the type of boss I would hope to be one day by watching her. She is patient, yet firm with her requests, kind and exact. She doesn't allow herself—or those who work for her—to be treated poorly by others or spoken down to. Surrounded even now by a staff of mostly women with a few dedicated men, she listens to their requests, takes their concerns seriously, and is fair in her responses. She takes a genuine interest in their lives and families and always wants them to go home at a reasonable hour, even though I am sure many nights they are too busy to.

One of the most important lessons I learned from her is the ability to never give up on one's passion. A second-grade teacher at heart, she has never left behind a mentorship attitude, even now in her new role as Second Lady. Her heart is filled with passion for art and teaching, and although she doesn't do these in traditional professional ways anymore, she has still found a way to be a part of them. Through her initiatives to bring awareness to art therapy, and her personal artwork on our children's book, she has continued to find ways in which to use her gifts as the Second Lady.

Since the election, she has visited art therapy programs, hospitals, and military bases, to name a few. On one particular overseas trip to Japan, we met with military spouses on the USS *Ronald Reagan*. She went around the room and shook hands with each spouse individually, then sat down at the table and opened up the conversation. She asked them to be honest with her and tell her in which areas they really needed help. I remember seeing their faces fill with gratitude as they told her of specific situations where they could use support. She took notes the whole time, as she always does in these types of meetings, and promised she and her staff would follow up soon.

When we left, I mentioned how moving it was to see them respond to her in this way. These military wives had been through much more than we had with their husbands deployed for months at a time, and yet, they were so touched by her response.

"It's not because of *me* as a person," she said to me. "It's the position. And for the short time I am in this position, I want to do as much good as I can." Mom takes the current role she is in seriously, as she does her role of "mom" and "wife." She is the strongest woman I know in her own right, and yet she is also one half of the strongest union I have ever known.

Traveling on the campaign trail with my parents allowed me to see their relationship up close in a different way than I had as a child growing up. They were still my parents, but I was able to admire them as leaders and partners, too.

At town hall events and rallies, Mom and Dad always held hands before stepping out into the spotlight and waving to the crowd. The audience cheered as they walked to the podium and Dad gave a thumbs-up to supporters. Mom quickly kissed him on the cheek before taking her seat with me in the front row. This was what everyone was able to see—the two of them onstage together and her watching attentively as he gave the speech she and I had heard countless times already. What people didn't see was backstage before they went out. Every single time, Mom whispered an encouraging word in Dad's ear. Oftentimes it was so quiet not even I could hear it. But he did.

Mom is her own person, but she is also fiercely one half of a pair, a marriage, a partnership. Her adept ability to balance these two concepts awes and inspires me each day. It is something I hope to emulate one day in my own life and I have been blessed to have her as my example.

Chapter Eighteen

Prioritize Your People

If you lose your family, nothing else will matter much.
—Dad, quoted in the book I wrote as a Father's Day gift
to him, The Lessons You Have Taught Me

I am proud to say I am one of the few women with whom Mike Pence dines alone.

Growing up, it was a tradition—and still is—for Dad to take me out to breakfast on the morning of my birthday. It started when I turned six years old and we had spent the week at a dude ranch in Colorado. There's a picture of me holding his hand, wearing cowboy boots and jeans, heading off to the restaurant. It was a big deal to have this time with just Dad and me. I remember opening my present, a new dress for my first day of kindergarten in a few months. In fact, we still have that dress somewhere up in our attic.

Dad and I have attempted to continue this tradition over the years, even as I have grown up and moved away.

On my nineteenth birthday, I remember wanting to rush through our breakfast at a local diner. I was a teenager, heading to college soon, and was a bit selfish in wanting to go hang out with my friends over him. I was struggling a bit with my relationships at

the time, and I didn't have a very high opinion of myself. I masked
this with pride, as so often happens. At the end of the breakfast,
I opened a card from him. He had handwritten a note to me on
the inside, saying how proud he was of me. He wrote that I was a
strong woman, with high standards who wouldn't settle for anything less than I deserved. I put the card away, ashamed, because
I did not think that was true. He could see it in me, though—the
potential to be better, to do better, and eventually, I would, too.

Dad has always had the ability to see the potential in other
people, especially staff members, and I have always been proud of
the way he has elevated women to levels of leadership in the workplace. It was through his lessons and example that I was raised to
believe I could do whatever I set my mind to—and be whatever I
wanted to be.

On the trail, Dad had a line in his stump speech that always
resonated with the crowd. "In America," he said, "anybody can be
anybody." He always paused before the last word and let the crowd
fill in the blank, before ending the sentence. In America, anybody
can be whomever they want to be. He would drive the point home
by saying it doesn't matter where you start in life—that if you work
hard, you can achieve your dreams in this country. As a little girl,
it never occurred to me I couldn't do something because of my
gender and this was a direct result of the kind of parents—and the
kind of dad—I had.

I am blessed to be in a family where my parents have been
married for more than thirty years but still look at each other as if
they met last week. I can't count the amount of times Dad tells me
something amazing Mom did. It's almost as if he is a friend of mine
who met this girl that I just *have* to meet, and I'm like, "Dad, yeah,
I know her. She's great. We're all on board. Mom is the best." But
he just can't stop bragging about her, and truthfully, I don't want
him to.

Families come in all shapes and sizes. There is no one way to create a family, but this one is my reference. I was born into it. I did not choose it, but I wouldn't ask for anything different. I can only comment on the type of family I have, and I can only celebrate the support, love, and devotion it has given me and encouraged me to have in my own life one day.

After the election, there was a story about one of Mom and Dad's practices in their marriage that came to be known as the "Pence Rule." It was discussed a bit on the news for a few days. Dad and I were up watching together one night when I decided to call it a night and go to bed, but as I was heading up the stairs, I felt like there was something else I needed to say. I headed back and sat on the edge of the couch.

"Dad," I said.

"Yeah?"

"Thank you."

"For what?"

"For only having dinner with my mom my entire life."

He smiled and I hugged him.

I hope that moment showed him that was all that mattered. His kid appreciated it. His daughter looked up to him and felt gratitude for him not having dinner with other women. At the end of the day, at the end of our lives, it only matters that we did what was right for the people who matter most.

The reasoning behind his decision is where the value is found. He put Mom first. He always puts her first, and he cherishes his relationship with her above pretty much everything else in the world.

So, maybe it is fine if we take criticism for putting those we love above anyone else.

Maybe it is more than fine.

3

Chapter Nineteen

Be That Friend

Hear the voice of love that's calling
There's a chair that waits for you
And a Friend who understands
Everything you're going through
  —Zach Williams, "To the Table"

We encounter people from all kinds of backgrounds, each a vivid character, every day. When I meet people for the first time, I try to take a moment to realize these people have pasts and histories and story arcs that led them to this moment. This helps me empathize with those with whom I may not have much in common. Whenever I discover something new about someone, something surprising, it always catches me and reminds me I have a very small piece of the entire picture.

The campaign trail was full of all sorts of interesting characters, those who are part of the story that lives on in history. From the supporters we met at rallies to the ones we worked with every day, each one had his or her own individual reasoning for supporting the Trump–Pence ticket and showing up in the way they did. It was a special time and place to be, but the lessons I learned from them along the way were the most important in shaping how I have viewed the world since then. It may seem as if there is little that can be taken from a presidential campaign trail and applied in real life, since the trail is so different and unique to its own world. This world is not all that different from yours. These characters, those who were part of the story of the campaign, may have different titles or positions, but in reality, they are just people, too.

Watching Dad and candidate Trump together was a lesson in friendship. People often commented on how different they were while we traveled across the country. On the trail, Dad openly welcomed this observation, and he felt there was something special in the connection the future president had with the American people. We had been in politics for years but had never seen this kind of enthusiasm.

Dad commented on this in his convention speech. "You know, he's a man known for a large personality, a colorful style and lots of charisma. And so, I guess he was just looking for some balance on the ticket."

They were different in their personalities and demeanors, and yet, they complemented each other in obvious and important ways on the campaign trail.

For me, it has been important to become friends with people who are different from me. They have different perspectives, since no two people on the planet have lived the same life or had the same experiences.

In my campaign trail notes, I wrote this in September 2016:

I have also learned so much about friendship through this experience and through watching my parents, especially my dad. He's my dad so I can't really call him my friend, but if he were not my dad, I would hope to be so lucky to have a friend like him.

I think people always say that in situations like this, when people are tested, you find out who your friends are. But what they don't tell you is that you find out who your good friends are. Anyone can have friends who stay or go, or come back when you're in the spotlight or when something good or bad happens to you, but it's really about discovering how those people see you after something like that happens.

I was very blessed to have friends who could travel with me for parts of the campaign trail. Some were supporters of the Trump–Pence ticket, and others were not. They are still my best friends to this day, and while they may have been afraid this new level of recognition would change me in some way, they showed up to see for themselves and supported me throughout the journey.

Upon first meeting people, I never assume they know who my family is, who my dad is. In fact, I don't tell them. This isn't because I am embarrassed or ashamed of my last name. Rather, it is because it genuinely does not come up.

It is not a natural (or, really, acceptable) flow of conversation to start discussing what one's parents do for a living out of the blue. This is really how I have always viewed it. I also do it for the story. It leaves the door open for people to find their own way in, which always happens in a fun and interesting way.

One of my friends who came on the campaign trail with me loves telling the story of how she and I were friends for months before she knew my dad was the governor of Indiana. I mentioned to her in conversation how my parents weren't allowed to drive themselves anymore, but failed to mention this was because of their security detail and not because they had had their licenses taken away. Instead of asking me why this was, she politely changed the subject and would put the pieces together later on when mutual friends told her the truth.

While I do actively withhold the details of my parents' jobs until others inquire, this isn't because I am embarrassed by them. To be completely transparent, though, it can be intimidating for me before people find out. Sometimes my own misperceptions about others can lead me to fear being treated differently once they know. I have realized, though, that it is just as bad for me to assume things about others, like what they think of my family, before having an interaction with them. Time and time again, the goodness of people proves me wrong and genuine conversations reveal common ground. When we connect on a human level, one-on-one, everything becomes clear once again.

If I walk into a room and immediately try to identify the people who may disagree or agree with me, that is a problem. If I do not enter every conversation with the notion that I may find common ground and a level of empathy and humanity, that is a problem. It is similar to overhearing gossip about someone at work and then forming an opinion of that person based only on hearsay that could have been taken out of context.

I believe I am at my best when I attempt to truly see the other person.

Policy does not equal personality.

Disagreements cannot lead to demonization.

I look forward to the day when commonality outshines polarity, when our friends are not people who agree with us about everything but rather challenge and encourage us to see a different point of view. I hope to see a day when upon meeting me, your curiosity is not based in a desire to uncover controversy but rather to discover the similarities between us. And I'll do the same with you.

I believe this day is coming.

I have to.

Chapter Twenty

———

Recall the Kindness

May I always ask questions and learn from those around me. May God grant me the ability not only to learn, but to remember the lessons.

—My Campaign Trail Journal, October 2016

There is a kind stranger in all of us. In the face of criticism, there is optimism to be found. The following story is dedicated to not only that fact, but also to a specific person: a man in the dining establishment of Cheeburger Cheeburger.

I have been known to steal shirts from Dad and Michael.

There is one shirt that is my absolute favorite. Technically, it does belong to my dad, but it was a gift from a stranger in the Cheeburger Cheeburger establishment of Sanibel Island, and it is to him that I write this letter of gratitude. I also direct my words to the hidden soul in all of us, the ability for each and every person to be unnecessarily kind.

My family has been going to Sanibel Island for thirty years, since before I was even born, and while there, visits to Cheeburger Cheeburger were a must. In fact, growing up, whenever we wanted burgers and fries for dinner, it was regularly indicated by us simply saying, "Cheeburger Cheeburger." This restaurant is a popular staple of Sanibel and the kind of place where there are photos of people on the wall who have completed the "Two Pounder Challenge" or "2.0 Challenge," where one eats two pounds of food consisting of a one-pound cheeseburger, plus a milkshake and fries. Whoever completes the "Two Pounder Challenge" is celebrated with bells, whistles, and, you guessed it, a T-shirt.

Sanibel has always been a place of recuperation for our family. The first time my parents went there was after Dad's father passed away in 1988. They returned when Dad lost his first election and we took trips there as a family while I was growing up. It was a comfortable little island for us, a peaceful place to return. After a few years and a couple career changes, Dad having become governor of Indiana and then vice president of the United States, our family found ourselves back in this restaurant, huddled up at a table in the corner. People were very respectful, and Dad couldn't resist waving to little kids who stared over at us (or who were more likely checking out the table of Secret Service agents nearby).

While we were eating, a ruckus suddenly broke out; there was laughter and applause, and we joined in to celebrate the person who had successfully completed the feat of the "Two Pounder Challenge." Later on, our meals were almost finished and milkshakes were on the way when our waiter (I remember his name was Mike, because I found this hilariously coincidental, but my brother had told me to "chill out") came over to let us know that the person who had won the Challenge wanted us to have his T-shirt. Mike set it down on our table, smiling, with a handwritten note on top.

We told him we couldn't possibly accept the man's trophy— or we at least had to get a picture with the champion, but Mike informed us he had already left. The note said they were a family from New York and wanted to give us this as a part of their appreciation.

It was simple. It was kind.

We finished our meal and took pictures with families who politely waited for us to finish. We left the restaurant and took our fifteen-car motorcade the two blocks back to where we were staying.

As we drove, I thought of all the families and kids Dad had taken pictures with that night. Most people stayed away while we were eating, but afterward, parents nervously nudged their children toward him and asked for a picture or an autograph.

Dad always makes a point to say, "Thank you for saying hello." He says this is because he wants people to know it's all right. Out of politeness, many people feel guilty for interrupting him when he is with family, but he always lets them know it's okay. It's funny to me, especially, because I know if the situation were reversed, our family would do the same thing. In fact, we did in the past.

When Dad was first elected to Congress, we met President George W. Bush at a retreat for congressional families. Michael scooted up to the front of the line with his sisters in tow behind and our parents close by. He handed the forty-third president of the United States a three-by-five note card and asked for his autograph. President Bush noticed Audrey and me standing behind Michael and asked, "Are you going to share this with your sisters?" We hesitated—we hadn't brought anything for him to sign. The president smiled and said, "I'll sign it three times, and you can cut it in thirds—one for each of you." My parents thanked him profusely, and needless to say, we did not cut it. It sits framed in our house—one note card, with the president's signature written three times.

A few days after our dinner in Sanibel, as we were packing up to leave, I spotted the Cheeburger Cheeburger T-shirt. "I Completed the Two-Pounder Challenge!" it proudly announced. Dad had set it down on a pile of items heading out to the car, and when I picked it up, I noticed it was enormous. It probably wouldn't even fit him, and it would be a dress on me. *Pajamas, perhaps?* Perfect. I tucked it away into my bag and we headed out.

As I write this, I don't know if he ever figured out I took it. To be honest, it is very much like me to steal his clothing, so he probably correctly assumed that's where it had gone. Yes, I do love stealing sweaters, T-shirts, and hoodies from my brother and father, but that isn't the reason I kept this one. I did so because I wanted to remember the act of kindness from a stranger expecting nothing in return. We never got to thank him; he didn't get a handshake, or an autograph, or a picture, even though all of those things combined would have been fine. He and his family just gave us this gift to be nice and I wanted to remember that.

I wear the T-shirt to clean in or after work when I want to change into something comfortable and loose. It's become one of my go-to items, actually. When I wear it, I am reminded of all the opportunities we have every day to do something out of the ordinary, unsolicited, and to just be nice for no reason other than the fact that we can affect someone's day, and therefore their life, for the better.

I hope one day this XXL gray-and-red T-shirt will be faded and well worn, having served me many days when I needed reminding of the simple, human sincerity in the world—and that is the true reason I took it—because I knew I would forget.

Chapter Twenty-One

See the Miracle

Love One Person, Deeply and Truly
—Dad, quoted in the book I wrote as a Father's Day gift
to him, The Lessons You Have Taught Me

Many people across the country and in the media were surprised by the results of the election, and ever since that day, I have honestly told people I was not. This is not because I was overly confident or sure we were going to win. It was because I was on the campaign trail, physically traveling along it with my parents, meeting the people who would show up to vote. I very well may have been just as surprised as everyone else had I not gone with my parents. If I had only seen the election unfold through the lens of the media, I surely would not have expected a win.

Rather, I was humbled by, in awe of, and grateful for the support of the American people and their vote for Donald Trump. I was not surprised, because I had seen them, I had talked to them, and I had come to know many of them. I saw the crowds who supported the Trump–Pence ticket and I had never seen anything like it. I had watched campaigns my entire life and had been an active

participant in them. I had never before seen the level of enthusiasm and excitement for a candidate as I witnessed for Donald
Trump.

One story in particular stands out to me. We were on one of
our many stops in Pennsylvania and had stopped at a restaurant
to meet with voters and invest in the local economy. Dad went
around to each of the tables, shaking hands and answering questions they had about policy, the candidate, and the country as a
whole. This is truly one of Dad's favorite things to do as a politician, if not *the* favorite thing—meeting with real people, talking
to them, and gaining their insight.

A family of about five people was waiting on the sidelines to
talk to Dad. I nudged his shoulder and he turned to them, shaking each of their hands individually. The woman of the group
stepped forward, telling him each of them had just absentee-voted
for Trump. Dad thanked them, and the woman continued her
story. She told us her father had been a manual laborer his entire
life and never voted in an election. He said there was never a
candidate worth voting for, and if one ever came alone, he would
vote.

She paused before continuing. "He passed away last month."

Dad held her hand and gave her his condolences.

She said, "He said Trump was the first candidate to ever come
along worth voting for. He was going to vote for him, but he never
got the chance to."

She gestured to her whole family behind her and smiled. "So
we all did for him."

Dad thanked her again and told her he would pass the story
along to Trump, which he did.

It is my belief that if you are going to run a race—any race—
you should run to win. This doesn't mean you should physically
harm yourself or push yourself to a limit that is not sustainable. It

simply means to put your best foot forward, to know you did your best, so you can feel good about finishing and going home.

. During the 2016 campaign trail, we ran to win.

I think everyone who enters into a presidential race does this, so I am not saying this is why we won. Supporters can tell whether or not you have faith in your own cause, in your own agenda, and in the movement they have created for you. Mom and Dad were ready for the next step and they ran the race wholeheartedly, never losing sight of the people who got us there, the people in the crowds at every rally, the people lining the street with signs when we drove to events. These people are the reason Donald Trump won. Their faith in him and his campaign's message led to a victory.

I have lived through quite a few election days, and each one is as nail-biting and miraculous as the next one. While you never go into an election day knowing for sure what will happen, I believe there is value in portraying confidence in your message, your team, and your supporters. It is similar to coaching a team before a big game. If the coach loses faith in the players, there is little chance they will muster up the belief themselves amidst the nerves and distractions.

Our team and our supporters were the players who would decide the outcome, and like athletes taking the field before a big game, the hardest part is waiting for it all to begin.

On November 8, 2016, we woke up, our bags packed for New York, and walked across the street to the little voting center in Indiana where we had cast our vote for years. It also happens to be the place where my parents first met, but more on that later.

I put my ballot in the machine as Dad stood behind me and watched it go in. I was nervous I would mess something up with the media all watching me. They asked if I had voted for my dad, to which I replied, "Yes." I have often thought back to that question—and been asked it many times since. I am not sure why the vote I decided to cast is more relevant than anyone else's. I know most people must think that if I had not voted for him, maybe that would mean I didn't support him or I disagreed with his politics. Truth be told, I don't agree with Dad on everything policy-related, and we have spirited, healthy debates about this. I am not a politician and it is my opinion that my political beliefs do not need to be publicly broadcasted. I understand that others would perhaps find it fascinating if I were to vote against him in an election. However, this would not be strange in my family. In fact, I believe it would be celebrated if I decided to do that. This is because our beliefs are our own. We do not have to agree with our parents in their politics, religion, or way of life. They encourage us to have our own opinions, yet to have an open mind toward theirs. This is the way in which I was raised. Being open-minded does not mean that you have to agree with everything, or disagree with everything, or have no opinion at all. It simply means you have to be curious. You have to be open to attempting to understand another point of view. Once someone's position is formed, you also need to respect their opinion and allow them to have it without being ashamed. This was not only encouraged in my family growing up, it was practiced.

After casting our votes, Dad spoke to the press and we walked back to the house to collect our luggage. Everything was set in motion, the plans that had been forming for months. The culmination of all the travel, speeches, and conversations with voters had led us here. This was it and it was their turn, the voters' time, to decide whether or not to put their faith in us. We drove away from the Indiana governor's residence and to the airport, waving goodbye to it, knowing that no matter what the results were, we would be returning to a different life.

That corner of Meridian and 46th Street in Indianapolis has

witnessed a lot of pivotal moments in the Pence family. As we drove away, I looked back over my shoulder and remembered all the times Dad had told me the story of when the most consequential, important, and beautiful event of his life had taken place:

It was 1983 and Dad had been visiting a friend on the north side of Indianapolis, near where the governor's residence is now located. The friend and his family attended a local church in the area, so Dad went along with them. That church is now the school building where we cast our vote that election day. It was there that he saw Mom for the first time, and nothing would ever be the same for him.

He had found his person.

She was singing on the altar in the guitar group and afterward, Dad followed her outside. They stood underneath a tree that still stands there today, and Dad has always made sure to point it out whenever we have walked by.

He walked up to introduce himself and told her a bit of a white lie.

"I'd like to play in the band."

"Well, you talk to that guy over there," Mom said, dismissing him and pointing to the worship leader.

Dad stuck out his hand, realizing he wouldn't get anything past this woman, and introduced himself.

"I'm Mike," he said.

"Karen." She shook his hand.

As the legend goes, Mom was holding her guitar in her left hand, so he couldn't see whether or not she was wearing a ring. This would lead to him doing everything in his power to track her down later.

They chatted and he found out her sister went to Indiana University School of Law in Indianapolis, just like him, and Mom was teaching art at a local elementary school.

Later that week, he called the school and told them he was working on the church directory and wasn't sure if it should say "Miss" or "Mrs." next to Mom's name. The woman on the other end of the line told him, "It's 'Miss.'"

Next, he had to find her.

He went to the registrar's office at the law school and asked the secretary for Mom's sister's number so he could get in contact with her. The woman let him know it was against the rules for her to give out students' personal information. Dejected, Dad turned to go, but just before leaving, he decided to go back and try one last time. He appealed to the woman's better nature, came clean, and told her he had met this woman who he couldn't stop thinking about, and he needed to get in touch with her.

The woman looked at him again and considered.

"Fine," she said. "But just invite me to the wedding."

And they did.

The story isn't over, though. As Dad was spending time with a friend later in the day, he went to a pay phone to call the number. That pay phone is gone, but it used to stand only a few blocks from the governor's residence.

Dad's hands shook as he dialed the number and his friend stood nearby waiting.

The phone rang and a voice answered.

"Hello?"

"Hi, I'd like to speak to Sheryl, please."

"She isn't here right now, but this is her sister, Karen."

Dad hung up the phone.

"What are you doing? What happened?" his friend implored.

"That was her."

"What do you mean?"

"That was *her*! That was Karen!"

"Well, what are you doing? Call her back!"

Dad called back, invited her to go ice-skating, and the rest is history. Mom says she knew after the first date she wanted to marry him. Dad knew the moment he laid eyes on her.

Some say love at first sight isn't real or realistic. It isn't realistic, but most miracles aren't; most things worth believing in aren't either. That doesn't mean we shouldn't believe they can happen. As Einstein said, "There are only two ways to live your life: as though nothing is a miracle or as though everything is a miracle." We have nothing to lose by believing.

Heading to the airport on Election Day 2016, I reflected on this. The physical street and building where Mom and Dad met changed over time. It became something different, something new, and people passing by today would never know the significance it had on my life. In a way, this was similar to election days as a whole. Every year, they come around and although they are similar in their traditions and regulations, the results they hold contain different levels of impact for different people. This is true for voters, candidates, and parties, but it is also true for families. We cheer on our coach, our mascot, our quarterback, who all happen to be the same person. We wait on the sidelines, on the edges of our seats, and watch with the knowledge that our lives will be different no matter what the outcome. Like the streets on which my parents met, we will change but we will never forget the events that happened there.

After we landed in New York City, we got settled into our hotel and tried to busy ourselves in the final hours the polls were still open. I remember working out in the hotel gym to get my mind off the results as they started coming in. The first state to go red was Indiana, and I smiled a bit to myself as I saw that, sending a mental thank-you to the Hoosiers back home. No matter what, they had said yes to us; the folks at home had sent us on to the next chapter, and that meant something.

The results continued to come in fast, but it would be hours before we knew anything substantial. I changed into my dress and took an extra-long time getting ready, trying to stretch out the minutes and distract myself. I even considered straightening my hair to give me something else to do. I gave up that idea and instead left it naturally curly, as is my habit.

We all loaded up in the cars and took the motorcade down the New York City streets to the headquarters at Trump Tower. This is something I will always remember—the activity of being involved in a massive line of cars and emergency vehicles, speeding down the often-crowded streets of Manhattan, with our way cleared before us.

We started in the basement of the headquarters, a bunker of sorts. It was where it all began and many of the same people who had once worked tirelessly at the roots there now busily monitored results upstairs. We joined them and said hello to everyone working so hard to process information, as they would be all night. There were television screens playing every news channel and as the final states started to be called, we went into the main room where all levels of staff were working. It was nothing fancy, no luxury suite with amenities. There were boxes of pizza for the staffers who would be there all night. This was where so many phone calls had been made, schedules had been set, and the grass roots of the campaign had formed. It was an honor to be in there with so many hardworking people, and we all stood around, watching the television screens together, waiting. The entire Trump family was there, too, including children and grandchildren. It was in this building where it all started, and here was where we would find out the results—all together, all with family.

States started being called for Trump–Pence, and many of the newscasters were shocked. People around us cheered when each was called, but nothing was to be celebrated yet. We had not won until the last electoral college point was tallied. Of course, that would go on much later into the night.

When they started reporting, there was no clear path ahead for the Clinton–Kaine team to win; people began to get excited. We called Audrey, who was still working abroad and watching the coverage, and said a prayer over the phone with her. Things were already starting to change, we could feel it, and we needed this moment—just the six of us, bowing our heads together. Just like that moment four years earlier, as we awaited the results of the Indiana gubernatorial election in the Lucas Oil Stadium bathroom, we clung to one another and held fast to our faith.

As some of the final states were closed, there was talk of a recount. There was the possibility of it being a long night, or the official announcement perhaps postponed until the morning, but we didn't want to go back to our hotel rooms, as we were unsure what was going to happen. Instead, we went to the Trumps' personal residence, where they wholeheartedly invited us to spend time as results continued to come in.

Once they called Pennsylvania, it was pretty much finished. I overheard Dad talking to Barron right after. It was a moving exchange. I wanted to remember everything I could from that night, so I jotted down the conversation in the notes section of my phone. Michael saw me do this and nodded his encouragement, perhaps sensing the end result of this book being written one day. Dad told Barron it was good for the country his dad was going to be president of the United States, and he thanked the youngest Trump "for letting us share this with you."

It was kind of Dad to say, and it was true. We had been invited on this incredible journey a few short months earlier. Our lives had been on one track up until July 2016, when everything had not just done a one-eighty, but a flip, roll-over, and dive into a completely different dimension. I, too, couldn't have been more grateful for the experiences we had been able to share with the Trump family. I would not have wanted to share it with anyone else. Their kindness, inclusion, and generosity was something I have tried to learn from and emulate in any capacity.

At around one in the morning, we decided it best to head over to the victory rally for the president-elect to give his acceptance speech. The Pence family had yet to eat, so some majestic staffers brought us snacks, which we scarfed in the car on the way over. Before we walked out onstage for Dad to do the introduction, I glanced at my family all lined up together. Audrey wasn't there in person, but we could still feel her presence and knew she would be watching.

The image holds steady in my mind of the crowd outside cheering beyond the curtain, excitedly awaiting their new president- and vice president–elect. They were ready for the acceptance speech, and my family stood ready to step out into the spotlight, into this new adventure, together.

Later on, after everything had settled down (or picked up, depending on how you viewed it), we were in our hotel room. It was around four in the morning. We ordered burgers and fries and were finally getting a chance to sit down. We watched the news coverage and chatted. I don't remember anything special we discussed. I thought about how in another life, this could have easily been us sitting up and talking about the results of the election like so many other families around the world. I wonder what our conversation would have been then, if we had watched the news as viewers and not as objects of the topics on which they were reporting. It may not have been much different, because as incredible as it is to be in a political family, it has never been the most important thing for us.

Of course, it is an honor and a privilege, but when it comes to the five (now six) of us, the most important piece of our lives has been our relationships with one another. No matter what life throws at us, we know there are these people to whom we can turn. As long as we remember and protect that philosophy, we will not only prevail, but we will also do so with the peace and knowledge that we have people in our corner.

Nobody was tired, but as election night was winding down, it was time to go to sleep for a few hours and get up to start our lives in this new reality. After an extensive, grueling interview process with the American people, Dad had been hired. This was his job now and I think he took comfort in that. The campaign trail is always an unknown road. Nobody knows what lies at the end of it. I don't think anyone should run for office simply for the thrill of the trail. If someone isn't confident in their ability to do the job, they shouldn't run. If I was sure of anything on the campaign trail, it was that Dad could do this job. He would be good at it. He would enjoy it.

As I went off to bed, he thanked me for coming along on the journey with them.

"Now the real work begins," he said.

He was right.

Chapter Twenty-Two

Pack Up, but Go Back

Fear not the specificities, and be yourself: It sounds easier than it is and it always, always will.

—My Campaign Trail Journal, November 2016

The house was to be put in boxes again.

It was late November 2016 and we were back in Indiana. When you win the vice presidency, there is an odd time of limbo called the "transition." This is the hardest part. I have learned a lot about transitions over the past few years and the main thing I know is they are never easy, although at times they appear to be from the outside. Times of uncertainty in a new place, often combined with a light schedule, can create an unhealthy mind-set. I found it important to engage in lots of intellectual stimulation in order to feel connected to the outside world.

We had a few weeks left in Indiana and were getting ready for Christmas, Michael's wedding, and moving back to D.C. I was working as a freelance consultant for a film company and enjoyed when I had projects to work on. I tend to struggle with downtime. It puts me in an off mood and I have to actively think through ways to busy myself. During this time, I became heavily invested in podcasts and writing my own personal projects. It was the first time I truly understood the world of podcasts and the ability to binge an entire season of *Serial*, walking around the house in a daze with headphones in, not wanting to miss a word. I listened to Guy Raz's *TED Radio Hour* and *How I Built This*, both of which inspired me to pursue my dreams and think outside the box. I listened to news programs and audiobooks while I went for runs at the gym or around our neighborhood. Podcasts connected me to the outside world when my family's newfound level of security kept me from venturing out as often as I used to. This wasn't because of any detail personnel in particular, but rather was due to my awkwardness in trying to understand the best way to get used to having this ever-present force around me.

While I did have downtime, there was also a lot to be done. Mom was working on packing up the attic and all our personal belongings. We had lived in the governor's residence for the past four years, so most of the furniture was not ours. The issue was we couldn't take any of it with us when we left. Our personal items had not been updated for twenty or thirty years, since my parents had first gotten furniture as a married couple. This meant we had all the small things to collect, and Mom did her best to organize in her elementary-school-teacher way with color-coded labels on boxes, which I am happy to say impressed the professional movers who came out to Indiana to pack us up.

The tradition is that the new Second Family is not supposed to move into the vice president's residence at the Naval Observatory until after the inauguration—actually, the day of the inauguration. This meant my siblings had never been inside our new home until after Dad was sworn in. The Bidens were kind enough to have my parents over for lunch ahead of time to show them around so they could start to plan whose room would be whose, and where the cat litter would go, and other important things like that.

My first encounter with Vice President Biden is one he is not aware of. I rode with my parents to their scheduled lunch with Vice President and Dr. Biden at the residence. Our motorcade pulled up to the house and circled around that front drive I have come to know so well, and there they were: the vice president and Second Lady, standing on the steps, ready to greet my parents. They did not know I was in the backseat of the car.

Dad said it would be fine for me to come inside and meet them, but I hadn't been invited and didn't feel comfortable barging in on their lunch. I waited outside as they ate and tried to catch a glimpse of their conversation from one of the windows, but it was no use. One of the Secret Service agents on our team offered to show me the property and so we walked around, it being my first time at the place that was going to be my home for the next year.

When they came back out the front doors, the vice president waved to the press and said something about welcoming Mom and Dad to the house. It was a good moment. He walked them to the car and I ducked down nervously, afraid he would see me cowering back there, fangirling.

I was embarrassed because I had worn jeans to the vice president's residence, and I felt it was disrespectful, so I stayed in the car until they were out of sight. I now believe he and Dr. Biden would not have cared in the slightest. They probably would have found it endearing and very "normal" of me. Looking back, it seems so silly to me now, as at this point I have lost count of all the times I have worn jeans in that house. After all, it is "my house," isn't it?

But it isn't.

Not really. I knew that then, and I still do.

I will always hold on to that feeling, that wonder and awe of national historic places and the foundation of this great country's tradition they represent.

Even now, when I enter the house or when I glance out the window near the staircase and see the National Cathedral in the distance, I take a few moments to take a breath and remember where I am.

In the day to day, it can be so easy to forget this is not my house, not in the slightest, and that is the beauty and sacrifice of public service in this country.

—⟨∞⟩—

There is an awkward overlap of time between when the governor of Indiana is inaugurated and the vice president is sworn in. This is the span of about two weeks, so essentially, Dad was unemployed for that time, and we needed somewhere to live. The new governor, Eric Holcomb, and his wife would be in charge of the Indiana governor's residence, so we were to stay in temporary housing in Maryland while we waited for January 20 to roll around.

Mom and I visited a few houses in Chevy Chase, Maryland, and picked one that seemed to fit our style of living. It was quaint and open, and we each had our own room for the inaugural weekend when everybody was in town. While we waited for that weekend, we mainly stayed inside or went into the Hill for meetings on the transition. I spent a lot of time writing and Mom and I discussed what our new life was going to be without having much idea at all. I didn't feel comfortable walking or running outside since we had been met with some protestors when we moved in, so I joined a gym and tried to stay active that way. I didn't feel unsafe, but I was still new to the concept of feeling watched and wanted to ease into it as much as possible.

Whenever we pull up to events and find protests going on outside, Dad always says, "That's what freedom looks like." He's right and I think he genuinely enjoys seeing people exercising their right to gather. Protestors impress me. I have known them, I have been one for different causes, and although it is strange to see people actively protesting the presence of someone you love, it is inspiring, too. This is because democracy is inspiring; freedom is inspiring, and even though something may evoke specific emotions in me, that doesn't mean it shouldn't exist.

During this time of transition, we lived in three different houses over the span of one month. I remember going over to a friend's house at the time and the shelves in her kitchen caught my eye. They were cluttered and stuffed with cookbooks, papers, knickknacks, extra clippings of notes long forgotten, memorabilia. I envied that clutter, that reality in which your home is a home that has been lived in. It had never truly felt that way for me growing up. With a parent in a job that could be taken away from them every other year with the election cycle, I felt as if we were constantly at the beginning of a potential start line, waiting for a gun that may or may not ever go off. My toe was always poised, my body ready, but it didn't happen for twelve years until we moved back home to Indiana to live in the governor's residence.

Then, after four years of my family living in a home that belonged to the state of Indiana and its people, we were heading out again. This time, it would be back to Washington, D.C.—the place to which we thought we had said our final goodbyes. I have been unbelievably blessed to live in such historic places, where my family has made its mark on history, something that I will probably not fully appreciate until I get to tell my grandchildren about it one day. I never had one home growing up, so I don't have an objective attachment to a certain place. Rather, home was—and is—people, togetherness, and love. These are the things that make up a home, that turn a house into a place we look forward to returning to. Of course, there are aspects of each house that I grew to enjoy and now find myself missing, but at the end of it all,

my family has stayed the same and our reliance upon one another
has been the foundation that has built us up and sustained us over
the years.

Still, I imagine myself returning to these places as an elderly
lady one day. I will take my children, and their children, on a tour
of the Indiana governor's residence. We will go through all the
regular motions of making an appointment as visitors. We will listen to the tour guide give historical details of the premises and
I will point out specific parts of the house where I know Mom
added her touch. I will retell the ghost stories, the legends, and the
memories of each room and corner. I will tell them how their great-
grandfather's favorite room was the study and there was never a
cold day when a fire was not lit and there was never a time when
his door was not open.

Chapter Twenty-Three

Hold Fast to Home

May the road rise up to meet you.
May the wind be always at your back.
May the sun shine warm upon your face;
the rains fall soft upon your fields
and until we meet again,
may God hold you in the palm of His hand.
—Gaelic blessing

There is a picture that has hung in our living room for as long as I can remember. As we packed up to move back to D.C., it was carefully wrapped for transport and now hangs in the vice president's residence. The picture is of a small farmhouse in Ireland, sitting in the midst of rolling hills and pastures. Below it reads Joshua 24:15: "As for me and my house, we will serve the Lord." The photo was taken from atop a hill, and the vantage point of the photographer was clearly a bit of a hike to get to. This photographer was Dad around the age of twenty and he took it when he visited the country of his family's origin after college.

He was supposed to take the trip with his grandfather, who

immigrated to the United States when he was a young man and drove a bus in Chicago the rest of his life. A few months before their trip, he passed away and Dad struggled with the decision of whether or not he should still go. They had planned it all out together—he was going to go along with his aunt and cousin and spend a few weeks working in Morrissey's Bar and Restaurant in Doonbeg, Ireland, a local spot still owned by our relatives. His dad told him he had to go, that even if it was not going to be the same trip he had hoped it would be, he still owed it to his grandfather to see where he had grown up. So Dad packed his bags and went.

He visited the small farmhouse where my great-grandfather had grown up. He saw the place where, as the legend in our family goes, his mother had given him a one-way ticket to America, looked west, and said, "You're going to America, because there's a future for you there." Dad snapped a picture of the house and framed it back in the States, so he would never forget the place he had come from.

In 2013, when Dad was governor of Indiana, we visited Ireland as a family over thirty years after Dad was first there in 1981. We set out to find the house. We had no address, no idea if it would even still be standing, but Dad remembered the area it was in, and the mountains to the east, and that was all we had to go on.

After about an hour of driving, we started to get hungry and were ready to call it a day. Dad was convinced we were going to find it, though, so we kept on. We turned a corner and something caught our eye. It wasn't the house, but rather a stone fence with a break in the middle. In the picture, there had been a similar fence in front of the house, with an iron gate in the middle of it. The house was gone, but there seemed to be a definitive area where it could have stood in the yard we found. The mountains were to the east, and everything seemed right.

I looked at Dad and asked if he thought this was it. Everyone agreed it had to be, but he wasn't sure.

"It sure looks like it," he said, but he seemed doubtful. He held up the picture to compare and looked over my shoulder to the hill behind me. It was directly across from where we believed the house to have once stood, and if it was the same place, it would have been right where Dad had taken that photo as a young man.

"I would have to be on the hill to know for sure," he said.

"So go," I told him, and decided I would join.

We checked it out. We'd need to hop a fence and scurry up the side of a hill where cows were grazing nearby. It seemed risky, especially since we had probably already created somewhat of a commotion by loitering in this small town for so long.

He seemed like he was about to do it, but at the last minute, decided against it. As we drove back toward the city, I was in the backseat, slightly fuming. This was probably an overreaction, but I felt as if he had let his fears and insecurities talk him out of climbing the hill. The threat didn't seem too great to me, and now he would never be sure if it was the same place.

He could tell I was mad, and when we stopped at a gas station for snacks and fuel, he asked me what was wrong.

"You wanted to go up. I know you did, and you let something else talk you out of it."

He considered this, knowing I was right.

When everybody got back in the car, he turned it around and headed back to the house.

"I'm going back," he said.

Objections rose from the backseat, but he shook his head.

"I have to know," he said. "I have to be sure we found it."

So, we drove all the way back down the country roads. He parked on the side of the road and we hopped the fence, traversing the wet Irish countryside together. As we neared the top of the hill, Mom drove the car up another side street so she could meet us at the top and we wouldn't have to roll down the hill to get back to the rest of them.

When we got to the top of that Irish hill, Dad held up the picture. I looked over at him and his eyes scanned back and forth from the photo to the land below. He smiled, traveling back in time.

"This is it," he said. "I'm sure of it."

He pointed at the mountains to the right of us.

"I was right here," he said, the excitement evident in his voice, like a little kid who had finally found a missing toy. "I snapped the picture from right here."

He pulled me into a side hug.

From this vantage point, we could see the spot where the house once stood. There was a clear area in the grass where the earth was different, the house having left some small indentation from the decades it had stood there.

We took another picture.

Now that photo hangs next to the one Dad took so many years ago. The new one is of Mom and Dad, broad smiles on their faces, and over their shoulder is a section of land my great-grandfather called home. His descendants returned to his birthplace together. Of all the accomplishments and honors our family experienced, this was the greatest. Capturing it was worth all the hard, small decisions we had made along the way.

Earlier in the week, before locating the place where my Irish ancestors had lived, we had traveled to different parts of the Irish countryside. Landing first in the town of Cork, we had rented a tiny European car and driven on the left side of the road through the lush, Irish country. We passed through Tubbercurry, the town where my great-grandmother had grown up, and made it all the way to County Clare, where we stopped to find my great-grandfather's land. We had encountered a few adventures already. At one point, I went for a run outside by the beach and got lost. My family searched for me for hours and I eventually had to cut through a golf course to find my way back to the main road and head home.

On one of our car rides, Dad had remarked about the last time he had come to Ireland as a young adult, unsure of where his future was headed. He had imagined himself returning to this island at some point in the far future and wondered if he would have lived out his big dreams by then. He wanted to serve as a congressman in Washington, D.C. It had always been a goal of his, ever since he was a small child. It never crossed his mind he would ever have the opportunity to be governor of Indiana, and certainly not to have the position he currently holds.

Upon returning to Ireland with us, he told me, "I am returning as governor of Indiana, to the country my grandfather emigrated from, and yet, that hasn't crossed my mind as much as the fact that my family is here with me. And I get to share it with all of you."

On the campaign trail, Dad commented on the history of his ancestors—and specifically, his Irish grandfather. He would tell the crowd how people would always ask him what he thought his grandfather would say if he was alive now—how he would respond to seeing his grandson as the vice presidential candidate of the United States.

Dad would bring the crowd's attention in by making a joke, saying, "Well, first, knowing me like he did as a young man, I think he would be very surprised." The crowd laughed, and Dad would pull them in closer by hushing his voice.

"But the truth is," he said, "I also think he would say that he was right. He was right about America. In this country, anybody can be anybody."

The day after the election, our relatives in Ireland hung a

"Make America Great Again" hat outside the door of their pub—the same one Dad worked in as a young man when he visited the land of his heritage for the first time. Underneath the hat, they had pinned a note that read "Gone celebrating."

Dad's success story—from lawyer, to congressman, to governor, to vice president—may prove that the American Dream is real, that it can happen, but it isn't the thing in life that has made him most proud. That would be us—and the fact that we are still intact and close as a family.

Dad had a saying in his early days as a politician he has carried throughout his career. He used to tell it to staffers who wanted to overbook him or plan something on the night of one of our birthdays. Mom would remind him of it when he was traveling too much or not spending enough time with each of us one-on-one. He lost sight of it sometimes, but that's where we came in, to remind him and bring him back. The saying was, "I'd rather lose an election than lose my family."

For us, this was an important saying, but actively living it out can be a challenge for any family. We have always worked hard to prioritize time spent together. It isn't always easy, but in order to stay grounded and maintain balance, we have always made a special effort to be together whenever possible and cherish the meaning of *home* from wherever we are. This is especially true for the holidays. The most frustrating times for us tend to be when it's not possible to be together or when visits are delayed. Christmas of 2006 was one such time. It was stressful for outside reasons, and as most objects of stress in life, the cause for the tension has long gone from my mind. I only remember how we dealt with it, and it has become a classic Pence family story.

It was December 23, and we had arrived a few days earlier from D.C. to spend the holidays at our little ranch house we kept in Columbus, Indiana. It had three bedrooms and was one level, positioned right at the edge of a soybean field with a hill we enjoyed climbing to catch lightning bugs in the summertime. The Flatrock River turned into a creek nearby, where we would swim and explore on hot days. At the time, though, everything was barren and covered with snow.

Dad hadn't arrived yet. Mom headed to the airport to pick him up. He was feeling down because he hadn't been with us until the day before Christmas Eve. He's big on Christmas, and I assume something such as voting schedules in Congress had kept him in D.C. until then. Growing up, for Dad and all of us, it didn't feel like Christmas until we were all together, and all in Indiana.

After Mom went to pick up Dad, Michael gathered the troops (that is, Audrey and me) and let us know we were all to come together and adorn the outside of the house with decorations, lights, and wreaths. We had it all in the garage, but since our trip home had been delayed, and Dad hadn't been there, the house lay bare and stood in darkness at the edge of the lane. This simply would not do for a Pence family Christmas.

We even found the fake tree and put it together, complete with a train running around the base. We hustled and got everything done as quickly as we could. It was freezing outside, but with one another's help, we did our best to reach the highest parts of the evergreen tree in the front yard and add lights to it and the bushes out front. Michael hung and lit the wreath, while Audrey and I filled each window with electric candles (Mom's favorite decorations).

They pulled up to the house just as we started to decorate the tree inside. Dad opened the door, his face in shock, and tears welled up in his eyes. He said he didn't even recognize the house from the outside because he had been expecting it to not have any lights. Mom hugged each of us individually. I told them it was all

Michael's idea, which he, of course, waved off. He insisted it was a group effort, and indeed, it was.

Dad walked around the house, commenting on each of the decorations as if he had never seen them before, like we hadn't been using these same materials every Christmas for the past decade. He was so proud. It meant the world to him we took the time to make Christmas special, even when we didn't have time, even when it wasn't convenient, and it would have been easier to just let this one go. That Christmas has often been relived by our family, in a way. Maybe not in exactly the same way, but there have been many times when we could have said we were too busy to live out our traditions, to make moments special, and to take the time to appreciate one another. We never did, though. It wasn't easy, but I have grown up watching my family make a conscious effort to go out of our way for one another, and each moment counts.

On another Christmas Eve spent at that house, Michael had just returned from his first semester of college and I had been missing our late-night talks together. Michael decided we should stay up late again, just like when we were kids waiting for Santa Claus to show up. He insisted I go outside and look at the stars with him. I lay on the ground, in the snow, with blankets wrapped around me, just talking with my brother. He told me about the different constellations and physics of space, his newest obsession as a physics major at Purdue University.

Orion's Belt always catches my eye. It is Dad's favorite constellation and it's one of the most recognizable in the sky, with its three dots right in a line. I have freckles on my leg in this shape, and at times, it has reminded me of the three kids in our family, all one unit, all combined.

I used to tease Dad about this, noting that it is the most recognizable of all the constellations, and so it is not original for him to say it is his favorite, as it could easily be everyone's favorite. He ignored this, as he should, and explained his reasoning I have come to agree with over time.

It is his favorite *because* it is so recognizable.

"I can see it from anywhere I am in the world," he said when I teased him.

He went on to explain the story behind the constellation, adding that Orion was a hunter in Greek mythology. If you look closely at the stars, you can make out his entire form, with arm raised in battle. Dad said it gave him courage no matter where he saw it. He has looked up and seen it in the Middle East, Europe, Asia, and all over America. It has traveled above him, sending a reminder to brave whatever feat lies before him, but afterward, to come home.

It gives Dad strength to know the same night sky he looks up at on one of his many travels is the same hanging above his family, even when he may be thousands of miles away from us. When he sees it at home, maybe he thinks of all the places he has been and the times Orion has watched over him and brought him safely back.

This concept of home is one that can be difficult to define. It can be a dream, an idea, a place, or a feeling. It constantly changes as we grow and move on in our lives. We may decide we want new things or struggle with accepting our past. I believe these are the times when home may be the most important notion to cling to. It does not have to be a perfect idea or a cookie-cutter concept. Home can be found in the most unexpected places—a kind gesture to a stranger or a good book at the end of a long day. We create home in the communities we build and the relationships we foster. This conviction guides me and points me back to where I came from even when I feel far away.

Some of those stories are included in this book, some will stay contained in our family, but wherever they end up, they will be shared. Their power and purpose is in their distribution. Their longevity happens in their ability to draw us together, year after year, and keep us afloat over time.

I often think of that little house in Indiana and of its stories. It is the center of lots of childhood memories for me, and when we eventually sold it after Dad became governor, I drove back for the first time by myself to see it. Another family was there, and I didn't think it would make me sad to see it newly occupied, but it did. We had all moved on in our lives, and better things were surely ahead for the Pences, but it was hard for me to accept that I needed to let go. Selling the house was representative of a time that was gone, a time that wasn't coming back. The memories are still real, though, and they carry us forward and help in times of transition. Memories remind us that these places and times we used to hold on to so strongly were once new ventures, too. There was a time when we were afraid to start fresh, and that fear turned into the amazing stories we will tell for years.

Chapter Twenty-Four

Then, Go Home

"It isn't Narnia, you know," sobbed Lucy. "It's you. We shan't
meet you there. And how can we live, never meeting you?"
"But you shall meet me, dear one," said Aslan.
"Are—are you there too, Sir?" said Edmund.
"I am," said Aslan. "But there I have another name. You must
learn to know me by that name. This was the very reason why
you were brought to Narnia, that by knowing me here for a
little, you may know me better there."

—*C. S. Lewis*, The Voyage of the Dawn Treader

My passion for stories began with my parents at a very young age. When the three of us kids were younger, we picked out a book series we wanted Dad to read to us. Every night before bed, he would do so. Mine was The Chronicles of Narnia, which has continued to be one of my favorite series of books even as an adult. I was enraptured by the myths and characters therein. The parallels between these books and the structures of Christianity recaptured my attention in college as I grew in my personal faith, and C. S. Lewis continues to be my favorite writer of all time.

While on our Ireland vacation, I worked through a collection of C. S. Lewis writings and my Christian faith became more real for me at that time. I would become a Christian a few years later in college after a trip to Israel, but this was when the stories and teachings began to become my own instead of the beliefs of my parents. On our trip in Ireland, I was physically lost for hours with my family out looking for me. It was a metaphor for my spiritual journey at the time. I was trying to navigate my way apart from the faith I had been raised in, and it was up to me to figure it out on my own. I needed to get lost in order to find the will to get back home, to discover what my personal beliefs were in adulthood.

When Dad read to me as a child, I first became attached to the fantasy world Lewis created, and then I returned to his theological writings when I found myself struggling with the parameters of faith in a complex and unjust world. The Narnia books are favorites of Dad's, too, and he still has his worn-out editions he read as a child in his office at home.

My parents were the first to see me as a writer, possibly even before I saw myself as such. As early as I can remember, I was telling stories. I would create games and made-up scenarios for Audrey and our friends in the neighborhood. I told long tales on car rides to my siblings, and at night, when Audrey had trouble sleeping, the room we shared for sixteen years was a perfect place for me to tell her stories to help her sleep. Dad always told me if I wanted to be a better writer, the most important thing was to be a reader. He and Mom instilled a love of the written word in me from a young age by reading to me and cultivating my passion for stories. He often joked that I would be the one to write his biography one day, and truthfully, that seems kind of likely now. I can only hope to have the opportunity to give him that.

My siblings and I are very different, and especially as we have gotten older, we have learned to rely on these differences when seeking out advice or a new perspective on a topic. My parents never saw any one of us having gifts any better or worse than another, and even when we pitted ourselves against one another, as siblings so often do, they never did. They celebrated that each one of our gifts were very different. Michael was athletic and enjoyed being part of a team, which ultimately led him to be an officer in the military. Audrey was a thinker and problem-solver, hence the lawyer route. I enjoyed more individual sports, or creative activities, which lent to my writing.

Navigating our desires and passions about what we want to do with our lives never really stops. As a younger kid, especially in high school and early college, I always knew I wanted to work in the film industry. I was convinced my desires and dreams would never change. However, as time has gone on, my dreams have taken on new shapes, but they are still rooted in the same characteristics my parents encouraged. I was never told what to do with my life, but I had the utmost encouragement and support to discover what it was that would make me the most fulfilled. By default, I was also taught to add something of substance to the world in my profession. This was never overtly stated, but it was reinforced by how my parents lived their own lives and navigated their callings.

While it may be thought that the way in which they served others most is through their roles in public life, they have really been doing this their entire lives. No matter what profession they have found themselves in, I believe they have fostered growth and encouraged the people around them in any way they can. They have added substance to the world more in their individual interactions with people than they did with any grand, sweeping titles. This is the most effective way to change the world—moment by moment, person by person.

Mom took every opportunity she had as a teacher to inspire

greatness in her students, to implore them to believe they could do anything they set their minds to. Dad acted similarly in his encounters with constituents, staff, and policymakers. We don't have to have an important title given by careers and positions in order to make a difference. We can do so each and every day with every person we see or with whom we speak. My parents changed our world by being good people and good parents. They always let us know we were valued, appreciated, and seen.

In regards to political life, the standing rule in the Pence family was that we kids were welcome at any and every event, but we were never required to attend. This meant we were free to choose. We could be as heavily involved as we wanted, and attend every meeting and every VIP reception and dinner, but if we wanted none of it, that was okay, too. My brother traveled a lot with Dad during his gubernatorial race, and I, clearly, was with them every step of the vice presidential campaign trail. In practicing this policy, my parents led by example with their staff and with the patrons we met. It showed the people around us that family came first, and it encouraged those who worked for us to put their families ahead of their careers, too, if they desired the freedom to do so.

Dad traveled a lot when he was in Congress, which could have easily resulted in our never seeing him. This potential scenario was not acceptable to my parents and so they came up with the idea to have the three of us take turns going with him. We would especially tag along when it was something that was of particular interest to one of us. Audrey went up to Chicago to see plays when she was interested in the theater. Michael attended a rocket launch at NASA, and I went along on a trip to Los Angeles when he visited a movie set. It was the first time I felt drawn to the city in which I now live.

He and Mom worked hard to expose us to experiences that would hopefully encourage and inspire us in our individual dreams.

They never pushed a certain idea, activity, or career path on any one of us. Instead, these conversations about what we wanted to do with our lives never included blunt statements. They asked questions; they wanted to know: What was it *we* wanted to do? How did *we* want to impact the world with our gifts?

Aside from his travel schedule, Dad also made the effort to hang out with us one-on-one, which for me, meant a day trip to New York City every now and then. Broadway was our favorite. We didn't go often, but from where we lived in D.C., we could take the bus up to the city, see a play, shop for Mom at the M&M's store, and take the bus back home later that night. In hindsight, this was pretty ambitious, but even though my middle-school self struggled to show my appreciation at the time, these trips were always something I looked forward to. It was Dad time, just he and I, our special thing.

Among the plays we saw were *Hairspray, Jersey Boys, Mamma Mia!*, and *In the Heights*. The weeks leading up to our trip, we would download the album and listen nonstop so we knew the songs before attending. It would be years later, after Dad was elected as vice president, that we would go to *Hamilton* together, naively assuming we'd have a similar experience at the theater, but it would turn into quite a different scene.

In late November of 2016, we were in New York City for a few days where Dad was working and he had a free night. He had the idea that we should go see a play, and I agreed. It was our tradition. So, we had our team make a few calls to see if we could purchase tickets. Most of the plays were sold out with such late notice, of course, and we had the option of a few. *Hamilton* was one of them, and I insisted. I'd heard so much about it, and never thought I'd get the opportunity to see it in person. I had heard stories of friends buying tickets months in advance and entering the "Broadway Lottery" every day to try and get a seat.

We went to dinner first with some family members and made our way over to the theater in our very conspicuous motorcade. When we arrived, the road had been temporarily blocked off and we hurried into a back entrance and waited. It is customary for us to wait until the audience has been seated and the lights are off, due to security protocol.

When we were given the all clear, we made our way through the venue and into the theater. However, the lights were not off and the entire audience saw us come in, Secret Service and all. People booed, cheered, jeered, and stood to applaud. It was the strangest cacophony I've ever heard and one of the weirdest experiences. I couldn't tell if people were for or against us, but we took our seats and enjoyed the show. We watched together, just like old times, but this time, I could feel every eye in the place on us.

When it was over, a few of the actors came onstage to address Dad as we made our way out of the building. This would go on to be heavily debated in the days to follow. My heart broke a little bit that night, but as the arts tend to do, they mended it again over time.

We haven't been back to a Broadway show yet, but I know we will one day. Dad and I will take a trip there together, and no matter what kind of reception we get, we will enjoy it. We will talk about the story, the lessons, and the music on the way home—just as we did with every play we saw together growing up, and just as we did after seeing *Hamilton*. We might be back on a bus or in a Secret Service vehicle, but either way, we will cherish each other's company above all. This was the greatest lesson I learned from all those times we went to New York City together. He was busy, probably busier than I will ever understand, and yet, he took the time, took an interest in me to let me know I was important, too.

Dad would often call me his "travel buddy" when we went on trips together when I was a kid. I came to realize the power of this statement later on in life—that this wasn't just a cute nickname. It held a lot of meaning. By stating this, he was letting me know that he not only wanted me to come along on his work trips with him, but he also needed me there. He often said this, telling me that I added value to the trip and I helped him. This is just another way Dad added dignity to my coming along—and he would do it years later on the campaign trail, too.

After one of those trips to New York City some years ago, we were sitting on the bus, headed back to D.C. It had been a long day and the four-hour ride was just beginning. I have a distinct memory of laying my head on Dad's shoulder as he pulled out our most recent Narnia book to read to me. He held it close to the window so he could see in the dim light, and began whispering so as not to disturb anyone around us. I closed my eyes, let the make-believe world wrap around me, and shortly fell asleep.

The fantasy world of Narnia was safer to me than the scary, outside reality with its uncertainties and unknowns. Sometimes, I still feel that way and look forward to escaping into books and stories in order to make sense of the real world.

I was lucky, though. I had real heroes in my life who existed beyond the pages of a book. I had characters, story lines, and parables to witness in person.

I had magic and I hope you do, too.

Chapter Twenty-Five

When You Can't Speak, Stand

And through it all you had each other. Just like we did.
—Letter from Jenna Bush Hager and Barbara Bush
to Sasha and Malia Obama

I am writing this exactly one year after the inauguration.

One thing I love about life is how unexpectedly it changes over time. Even when we think we know what the future will hold, opportunities come up and we may find our lives headed in an entirely new direction. When I take a moment to look back at the past and consider where I am and how far I have come, it astounds me to acknowledge how little I know of the grand plan. It's important to remember that the courses of our lives are not set in stone. We can adapt and mold them if we find ourselves at a standstill. When I feel trapped or lost, Dad tells me to reach out to different people and try new things. "That way, you make room for God to come in and lead you in the direction He may want for you."

While it is important to do this in the present day, it also helps to look back every now and then—to look at the places we have gone, and to see the people we have been.

I have a five-year journal in which I write one sentence every day. I started doing this a year ago, and it excites me to know I will have a five-year record of my life and how it has changed. I have just come upon a year, and I am now able to read each night the statement I wrote the previous year. This can be strange, as I have seen how my personal relationships have morphed so much. However, it is also invigorating to think how, a year ago, I was spending my first night at the vice president's residence in Washington, D.C., with my family having just been officially instated into this new role.

Inauguration weekend was one of those weekends that seems to go by in a blur and drag on at the same time. I wanted to take everything in, but I also wanted it to be over so we could get settled into our new life. I needed to make sure that my family was all right and that my parents were rested. I was protective of them each and every step of the way, just as I had been on the trail. I eventually learned that I needed to back off a bit, let them breathe, and live my own life. That weekend, though, I was still performing in my all-in caretaker-daughter mode and I was intent on everything going smoothly.

While this was my goal, I also wanted them to take it in. I hoped Dad would take a step back, breathe, and let the moments hit him. I don't know if you really can in a scenario like that. You take it one step at a time and you look up when you're through. Still, I hope he let a scene take his breath away every now and then. I think he did.

One moment in particular that did this for me was when my siblings and I were announced as we walked out of the Capitol and onto the stage. For some reason, I didn't think we would be going down the same corridors that Dad and the president would be going down, but we did. There were rows of military personnel, all saluting, and the hall was silent leading out to the open platform. Our names were announced one by one, and we walked out single file. The crowd was massive, and as the cold air hit my face, I tried to remember to smile. I wanted to turn around, grab Audrey's hand, who was walking behind me, but I looked straight ahead and found my seat.

I have been to a few inaugurations in my lifetime. I went to both of President Bush's and both of President Obama's. I couldn't miss them. I remember going to President Obama's 2008 ceremony with my brother, wading through the crowds to get to our seats. We never actually found them and ended up standing in a nearby area on the National Mall. There were so many people and they were so excited. It was a moving experience and one I wouldn't have missed for anything. To see the reality of American history unfolding that day was more than I can put into words. I was lucky to be able to see the first African American president inaugurated, and I will forever remember how special it was to witness.

The night before Dad's inauguration, I stayed up late talking to Michael about democracy. We commented that the inaugural ceremony is an amazing and wonderful thing. In truth, it is entirely contrary to human nature. Michael told me his favorite part is always watching the helicopter fly away because this is the moment the transition of power takes place. The most powerful position in the world is one moment held by someone, and in the next, with a vote from the people and an oath sworn, a new person is in that position. It is entirely contrary to human nature, to give up power at the will of the people. It is done voluntarily, yet the tradition of it is never guaranteed. We must insist upon it with every new generation. Democracy exists, freedom prevails, because we fight for it. We have the power, as the people, to ensure its continuance. We have the responsibility to do so.

After the official swearing-in ceremony, there is a luncheon in Statuary Hall. I always liked this room in the Capitol, because on a normal day, when it is not filled with tables and chairs, you can whisper on one side and be heard clearly on the other, a little bit of magic in our halls of government. When I was a kid, Dad never missed an opportunity to demonstrate this when we walked through the Capitol on the way to a vote or back to his office. It is important to not lose the childlike fascination with the secrets of the building, and to his credit, Dad never has.

Before the luncheon started, we were ushered into the room. It was filled with United States government dignitaries and world leaders. Everywhere I turned was a new person I recognized from newspapers, television, and the like. Former presidents and First Ladies were dining there and I was in awe at how normal it all looked—just another fund-raiser or dinner I had attended, but with people I had learned about in history books my entire life. I wouldn't have been all that surprised if one of the statues of American founders had come to life, hopped down off the pedestal, and taken a seat at my table to eat with me.

I glanced across the room and saw Secretary Hillary Clinton standing up, chatting with a crowd that had formed around her. I watched in awe. I had never seen her so close before. The only other time I had seen her in person was when I attended the first presidential debate in Las Vegas. At that time, she had been onstage, distant, and something about the atmosphere of a debate made me feel like I was watching from my television at home. In the Capitol, she was a real person.

My sister said we should go introduce ourselves, so I followed, trying not to act too starstruck. People had come up to Dad in the same way my entire life. I was used to being on the other side of it and witnessing the exchange from that perspective.

I waited behind a few people and when it was my turn, she turned and looked directly at me. I remember this because there was a man to my left and she didn't turn to him first; she turned to me. This may seem like a small gesture, something discreet and insignificant. However, many women reading this will perhaps understand it better than the men, simply due to the fact that when you are often in the minority, these actions stand out more. As many women know, it is more common for men to be addressed first in a group—even when the addresser is a woman. It isn't necessarily something done on purpose, and I am sure I have done it many times in the past, but it is noticeable when the opposite is performed, as was done in this case. All I know is that the former First Lady looked at me first—and that meant a lot.

I thanked her for her service, and she asked my name. When I told her, she said, "I have a granddaughter named Charlotte."

I fought the urge to say, "I know," even though I did.

She took an interest in me, asked what I was doing and where I had gone to school. She didn't rush through our encounter, and as I walked back to my table, I couldn't shake the experience from my mind.

I thought about it the rest of the day and have considered it many times since.

She could have been rude to me. She could have dismissed me with her tone or the way she spoke, but she didn't do that. Instead, she took me seriously as an individual person, and honestly, not many people do that. Of all people, she would have been somewhat justified in being curt to me, but she was not.

I cannot imagine how it must feel to serve in public life the way she has. People may assume I should be able to imagine this, since I am in a political family. However, being a political spouse, a First Lady, a senator, serving in a president's cabinet, and then being a presidential candidate is an entirely separate level of commitment to serving one's country. It ought to be appreciated, no matter what political affiliation one may have. Watching my parents do it is one thing, but actually being the object of the country's approval or disapproval is something else entirely.

In the days before the inauguration, the Bush twins read a letter they wrote to the Obama sisters. They did this when Obama
was first elected, and now they were doing it to say goodbye as the
girls headed out of the White House. They read it aloud on *Good
Morning America* and it caught my ear as I made breakfast in the
kitchen. I felt like they were speaking right to me as they read it,
and it is excerpted below:

> *Malia and Sasha,*
>   *Now you are about to join another rarified club, one of
> former first children—a position you didn't seek and one with
> no guidelines. But you have so much to look forward to. You
> will be writing the story of your lives, beyond the shadow of
> your famous parents, yet you will always carry with you the
> experiences of the past eight years . . .*
>   *You have lived through the unbelievable pressure of the
> White House. You have listened to harsh criticism of your
> parents by people who had never even met them. You stood
> by as your precious parents were reduced to headlines. Your
> parents, who put you first and who not only showed you but
> gave you the world. As always, they will be rooting for you as
> you begin your next chapter. And so will we.**

When they were done reading, I couldn't help but feel a catch
in my throat. I wasn't a first daughter, but I would come to understand more all the things they were talking about—the constant
presence of Secret Service, the verbal attacks on family members,

---

* *The Bush Sisters Wrote the Obama Girls a Letter*, Barbara Bush and Jenna Bush
Hager, quoted from airing on *Good Morning America*, January 2017, and published by *TIME* magazine, January 2017. http://time.com/4632036/bush-sisters
-obama-sisters/. Accessed March 2018.

and the silly, small tabloid stories. I had already gotten some much-needed advice from people who had been in my position before. When it comes to kids of politicians, the Bush girls were right—it is a small club and I have taken all the advice and help offered to me.

The show went to commercial and Dad, who had been watching, turned to look at me.

He had a knowing look in his eye as he put his arm around my shoulder. I think he could tell the letter had made me emotional.

"You know a little of what they're talking about, don't you?" he asked.

I nodded into his arm.

I did.

Families make sacrifices and no one knows this better than the politicians asking them to do so. The biggest sacrifice isn't the change in lifestyle or the added security or the awkward name recognition ("Are you related to *that* Pence?"), and the Bush girls got it right. I have often thought back to the one line that stood out to me the most in their letter:

> *You have listened to harsh criticism of your parents by people who had never even met them. You stood by as your precious parents were reduced to headlines.*

This is the strangest part of being in a political family. This is the biggest sacrifice. When someone says something mean about me, I am able to shrug it off and move on. If someone says something mean about somebody I love, it is an entirely different emotional reaction. This happens to everyone, and it doesn't matter if your dad is the vice president, or a teacher, or a farmer. If you have a good relationship with him, then you will be defensive when someone does something that has the capacity to hurt him. The role of a politician's kid, then, is oftentimes reduced to quietly fuming and "standing by" as they are "reduced to headlines." We can find help, and strength, in the knowledge that even though we may have to be silent about our disapproval in how they are sometimes treated, we still stand beside them when things are hard. Perhaps our support is not found in anything vocal we may be able to say, but rather in our presence and our persistence to stand. My parents consistently thanked me for coming along with them on the campaign trail in 2016, but I never hesitated. Sitting out on the porch at the governor's cabin in southern Indiana, when they first mentioned to me this may be a possibility, I immediately responded.

"Well, I would go with you," I said.

And that was that. I never considered it would be any other way.

When a politician enters into the public sphere, the entire family signs up. We all serve, but we don't do alone—and neither does the politician. The family members need one another, and the political figure needs his or her family by their side, even when "standing by" is the only thing—and the hardest thing—to do.

On the day of the inauguration, as Dad took his oath of office, his voice caught on the last words: "So help me God." I think maybe it hit him right then. Maybe he felt the weight of the last few months and next years culminating on those words. It was a declaration, an admission he would not be able to do it without assistance. This addition to the oath is an important one, and in my opinion, it makes it what it is. The oath-taker swears to the country, the voters, the citizens, that he or she will uphold the constitution, but that isn't where it ends. The founders included this essential phrase in order to ensure the oath-taker asked God for help, knowing full well he or she would not be able to do the task alone.

From me to the next family:

To everyone who will come after us—to all the kids,
grandkids, husbands, and wives who will know what it is like:

I hope you wear jeans, run in the hallways, swing from the
tree swing, and read the plaque: "To Jill, From Joe. Valentine's
Day 2011." Take long walks on the grounds, and through
the brush and trees. It will make you feel as if you live in the
woods.

Tell the vice president to drive the golf carts around.
(Secret Service is kind of okay with this.)

Talk. Argue. Make up. Keep calling each other.

Make it your own, enjoy it, for it will not be yours for long.
And there is wonder to be found in that.

As Michelle Obama told me onstage after the
inauguration, "Hold tight to each other. You're all you have
now."

Take a moment every now and then to look around and
ask yourself what your six-year-old self would say if he or she
could see you now. I don't mean this in reference to life as the
Second Family of the United States. I mean—you. Are you
living your dreams? Are you climbing your own mountain?

If not, change course.

Write your own story.

And never forget the heroes you meet along the way.

Chapter Twenty-Six

Let Your Faith Be a Uniting Force

I have learned so much about this experience—how to trust God, how to surround yourself with the right people, how to command with grace and patience and kindness. I pray I will be able to use that. I pray I will know when and how.

—My Campaign Trail Journal, November 2016

My personal faith journey points to my family's first trip to Israel. My visit there brought my faith to life for me. It became real. I was twenty-one years old and had been studying at the University of Oxford for a semester. I met my family in Israel for Christmas over the holiday break, before returning to England to finish out my year of studying abroad.

I heard about Israel a lot growing up from all the Bible stories in Sunday school and growing up in a conservative Christian household. Yet, the act of going there did something new for me. I realized most people there believe the events of the Bible did in fact take place. In secular Western culture, whenever I encountered people who were not religious or had no interest in Christianity, it always felt like they were saying the Bible wasn't true, that there was no proof. They said it was just a book filled with stories and myths. In Israel, it was different. No matter what religion a person in Israel might practice, I found that for the most part, they acknowledge the truth of the history of the Bible. They recognize the events took place. They just don't necessarily agree on all the details.

I felt a serious camaraderie and connection with these people. It was as if we were all on the same journey, and we had converged on one path for a particular point in time. I walked down that path and listened to their stories and experiences. We discussed the importance of faith in each of our lives and found commonality in our shared traditions.

I felt this again when we traveled to Asia for Dad's first trip to the region as vice president. In the middle of the ten-day swing, we found ourselves in Jakarta, Indonesia, meeting with faith leaders. My favorite moment happened there—in a conference room in the basement of the Istiqlal Mosque in the heart of the city.

Gathered were imams, nuns, priests, pastors, rabbis, and spiritual counselors. I put headphones on so I could hear the translation of each member of the group. A booth in the back of the room was filled with translators who actively translated the language of the person speaking to the language of the listener. Across wavelengths, we transmitted our messages through these translators and on to one another. The Muslim woman leading the discussion described her country as a place where all faiths are celebrated and I could tell from her interactions with the other leaders in the room that this was true. The people there were her friends. She spoke of the times they reached out to one another to discuss issues facing Jakarta and relied on the collective wisdom and connections to solve problems.

When we arrived that morning at the mosque, an imam met us and gave us a tour. He made sure we went to a specific spot where the parish next door was visible. He said he showed President

Obama the same spot and insisted we get a picture, so we could remember. He acknowledged our religion was different from his, and this small act of kindness is something I believe we can all learn from, in whatever setting we find ourselves.

Back at the meeting in Jakarta, Dad spoke to the group of men and women faith leaders. Smiling at the faces looking up at him, he said, "We celebrate that faith unites; it does not divide." Although it's hard to accept this at times, it is an important fact to hold fast to.

When people of different faiths gather, there can be a temptation to withhold one's views or close one's self off to the beliefs of another. The only way to combat this is to spend as much time sharing as listening. Instead of being afraid of the conflict that may come when people of different faith backgrounds are gathered, we must speak aloud the celebration of coming together. We must also allow ourselves to become excited not by finding people who agree with our exact way of thinking, but by encountering those souls who choose to believe something different.

When traveling to the Holy Land of Israel, it is common to hire an Israeli guide. It is helpful to have someone who can speak Hebrew and act as not only a resource on tours, but also provide the occasional restaurant suggestion. Ours was Roni. He has become quite a classic character in my family's stories and wisdoms we try and impart upon one another that are oftentimes stolen from (and accredited to) Roni. One of our favorite phrases of the trip was what seemed to be a tag line of his: "Roni says…" Whenever letting us know specific instructions or offering a piece of advice, he began with "Roni says…" and it became an often-quoted saying around our house.

One of these lovely "Roni says" pieces of wisdom comes to mind when I think about different religions in Israel.

It was a particularly warm day and we were walking on the edge of the city of Jerusalem. Roni pointed to the Mount of Olives

where many people are buried. This is the place where it is fore-
told the Messiah will come—for Christians, where Jesus will come
back. He pointed out the many Jewish gravesites on the side of
it, piled high with stones from visitors. It is common for Jewish
people to want to be buried on the Mount of Olives, since they
believe the Messiah will come here first.

Roni said a particular piece of wisdom to me on that hillside:
"It is believed this is where the Messiah will come back. When he
comes, we will ask him, 'Have you been here before?' If he says yes,
we'll know the Christians were right. If he says no, we'll know the
Jews were right. And that will be that."

I smiled at him and turned back to the hill. Maybe it really will
be that; maybe it could be just as simple as that.

I believe it was my time spent in Israel where I truly became a
Christian, where my faith was solidified for me. I had always had
faith, but it became my own there and I have never really turned
back since coming into this realization. It happened when I least
expected it. It was a time in my life I had turned away from God,
not wanting anything to do with religion. I was floating on my
own and thought I was fine.

I had become interested in atheism and spent much of the year
reading from thought leaders in this area. I was interested in other
types of ideas, ones I had not been raised with. I stopped going
to church and reading my Bible. I avoided religious friends and
felt that I wanted to do life without God. I believed I didn't need
Him, but as the year went on, I felt increasingly hopeless. I think
I still believed in God, but I wanted to try living without the burden of religious ideas. I thought my questions would go away or be
answered. I thought maybe I would no longer care and I would be
able to live in an agnostic way. Maybe a part of me even wished I
could, but atheism didn't answer any questions I had. It just left me
with more.

A few months after our holiday trip, I returned to God, asked for forgiveness, and felt Him accept me back. I was on a plane, listening to a religious song, and I began to cry. In that moment, I came home to my Savior, to my friend. I understood. I needed Him and He took me back in with open arms.

This incredible feeling of acceptance and renewal is one I cannot put into words, I cannot re-create, I cannot justify. It just is. It is a free gift, and one I cannot live without. And I have never been more sure of anything.

Chapter Twenty-Seven

Play to Beat Yourself

And we will not fear the moment before the lights go on . . .
—My Campaign Trail Journal, October 2016

Travels with Dad have brought me around the country and the world. I have seen so many incredible places and have met amazing people. As I have grown up, these trips have become less common and available with my work schedule. The last one I was able to go on was a ten-day trip to Asia. Our first stop was in South Korea, a place Dad had never been. He felt a connection to the country already, because my grandfather—his father—fought in the Korean War before Dad was born.

I never met my paternal grandfather, but I have heard stories about him my entire life. He lit up a room the moment he walked in. He always had firm advice and was a strong salesman and hard worker. His presence was missed when he was not there and overtly felt when he was. Even after his death, it seems as if his spirit still lingers in our family.

As our plane landed in the rainy, cloudy city of Seoul, Dad sat close to the window and peered outside. This was a common practice of his and not entirely out of the ordinary. He often likes looking out the window as we land, taking any opportunity to wave at the civilians, government, and medical personnel gathered. His body stayed turned toward the window as we taxied to the area where we were set to disembark. Stairs would be rolled up for us to walk down and we would most likely be met by members of the embassy. Everyone started preparing to unload while Dad stayed deep in thought.

He turned to me and I saw the emotion written on his face.

"He suffered here," he said, and I knew he was talking about his dad.

The stories I heard about my grandfather include anecdotes from when he was raising his six children and how he always taught them to work their hardest and do their best. He felt strongly about never performing for anyone else's approval, but rather to do one's best for the sake of that alone. He gave chances to his employees and always extended a fair deal. He was the one to coin the phrase "Climb your own mountain" in our family, telling it to his children as we were growing up. Do things the way you want to do them, work your hardest, and pave your own way.

On the campaign trail, I remember Dad talking to a young boy in Ohio who was participating in a golf championship that weekend. He seemed nervous and Dad told him, "Just beat yourself. That's what my dad always told me." This standard may seem easy to people who live trying to beat others, but the reality is that it is much more difficult and all the more rewarding. When you only compete against yourself, you are happy with the end result as long as you did your best. It doesn't matter if you get the approval of others in the process.

Dad passed his own father's advice on to me by way of a story when I was starting out on my own this year. My grandfather, "Poppa Pence," as we call him, owned gas stations in southern Indiana. One summer, Dad got a job working at a local station.

Everyone knew his dad owned the place and they weren't particularly friendly to him when he started. Nobody was outwardly rude, but they didn't want him to get special treatment just because he was the boss's kid.

Dad was upset about this one day, finding it hard to break through with the team and make connections with them. He complained about it to his dad, who shrugged.

"Just outwork them," he said. "That's how you prove yourself. Be the hardest worker there."

So he did. He showed up first and left late. He volunteered for all the manual labor jobs and was the first to put in more hours.

When I moved out this past year, Dad told me this story. I was finding my way, trying to figure out how to be my own person within my industry. It was nothing new to me, but I did want to make it on my own and Dad understood this better than anyone.

I never wanted anyone to think I had been given a handout. Of course, I had connections that other people don't have and I am blessed with experiences that led me to this place at the beginning stages of my career. I still wanted to do it on my own, though, and Poppa Pence's words helped me figure out how. I never grew up feeling as if I did not know him. Even though we never met, it feels like we did and sometimes I even dream of speaking with him.

While there are many stories about him I can retell from memory, there are also those anecdotes I did not hear. These were from his time spent in the Korean War. I never heard them because he didn't tell them.

Dad often comments on this in his speeches, saying that his dad came home with medals that were put away in a drawer, never to be spoken of again. He was awarded a Bronze Star for leading his platoon across a minefield. He walked in front of them to test the ground first and make sure it was safe. From what I have learned about him, he wasn't interested in praise and probably didn't think he deserved the recognition. When speaking to veterans and military officers, Dad talks about this in regards to his father. My grandfather's cousin always said that he "never got over the guilt of coming home." The crowd of mostly vets always nods at this part, understanding something I probably never will.

Upon our arrival in South Korea, I think Dad felt a physical reaction to being in a place where his father had struggled so much. It was almost as if he could somehow feel the fear and pain his dad had experienced.

Although it may be painful, I believe it is important to visit the places our family members have been. My grandfather's experiences shaped him, which contributed to how he raised his son, who then raised me. By default, and over the ages, I am connected to this place, too. We should actively engage in the areas that hold good memories for our ancestors, but we should also go to the painful places, the ones that shaped them into who they became. It helps us to empathize with who they were and to understand better who we are.

One of the most memorable experiences of our trip to South Korea was when we went to the demilitarized zone, the line dividing North and South Korea. We took a helicopter across the country and then drove in bulky vans through the hillsides, where we entered the military complex. There were Korean and American troops, walking side by side, chatting and carrying supplies to nearby areas outside. These were the men and women physically defending the border, on constant watch every day.

We went inside a building and into one of the conference rooms. There were name cards for where we were to sit and a few of the head officers waved us in. One of them was Korean, and through a translator, he welcomed us to the base. He showed us a video and pamphlet about the history of the area they prepared in advance. They had done research determining where my grandfather fought, which battles he was involved in, and they outlined this for us in detail.

I could tell Dad was so grateful for this, finally able to put facts with the stories he had heard snippets of his entire life. We walked around the building a bit, then got back into the vans to head to the edge of the border, a short drive away. It was raining when we arrived, and I walked behind Mom, holding my hand out to steady her back. We had been warned in advance not to wear shoes that would be difficult to walk in and I was grateful for this bit of advice.

When we got to the top, a decorated military general traveling with us pointed over the edge of the wall where we stood. He told us that Pork Chop Hill was in that direction—the place where my grandfather had fought one of the key battles in the Korean War.

It was foggy, damp, and eerie. I squinted into North Korea and tried to see as much as I could. It was silent but for the music blaring on loudspeakers. I asked what that was for, and the general told me it plays constant propaganda in Korean, telling South Koreans to defect to North Korea and denouncing the United States. It is a beckoning and a warning.

We took the military helicopter back to where we were staying and went to our hotel. Our evenings were mostly free, thanks to Mom, who is the ultimate protector of rest on long trips such as these. I sat in our hotel room with a lot of time to think about the day and the significance of what we had witnessed. Of course it was historically notable, but it had also been a meaningful day to our family personally. After all, Dad returned to the place his own father left. My grandfather physically, and literally, fought for peace in the region during the Korean War. He left best friends and comrades behind when he returned to America, and maybe he tried to leave behind the memories, too, but I am never sure that works, as hard as we may try.

He went home, started a family, and did his best to move on.

Decades later, his family came back to live out his legacy. Dad is not in the military; but he returned to South Korea, fighting for freedom and peace, too. Time will tell how the events of our present play out in the future. We play the game to beat ourselves even when it seems as if we are playing against the world.

Chapter Twenty-Eight

Find the Object of Your Gaze

You raise me up, so I can stand on mountains.
You raise me up to walk on stormy seas.
I am strong when I am on your shoulders.
You raise me up to more than I can be.

—Josh Groban, "You Raise Me Up"

There is already a committee planning the president's funeral.

We found this out after the inauguration. I remember Mom commenting on this to me, saying a group had been formed already to plan the event in full. State funerals are massive events that take years of planning. It makes perfect sense that an entire committee would be needed to plan one, but it still feels strange to the family members.

When I was a kid, I had Dad sign a paper acknowledging he wanted "You Raise Me Up" by Josh Groban played at his funeral. It is his favorite song and he often returns to it when he is in need of a reminder of God's presence.

For some reason, as a child, I was very concerned Dad's final wishes were going to be overlooked. As an adult, I realize this was a little silly and it wouldn't be as big of a battle to get this song played at his funeral. Most people who know him closely are aware of his connection to it. My obsession with this showed my dedication to the integrity of his memory at a young age.

A tangible way in which Dad's memory will be preserved exists in the form of a painting in the Indiana State House. This is the governor portrait.

When it came time for it to be painted, Dad was faced with some decisions regarding the process. One of these was whom he would choose to paint it. He met with a handful of people individually—esteemed painters, artists who had spent their careers celebrated in museums, and many who had worked extensively with high-level clients. The last painter he met was a man from southern Indiana. He was a talented artist and so excited and honored by the possibility of even being considered. When it came down to it, of course Dad chose him—the one from small beginnings, the one who didn't expect to get the job.

He and his wife came to the Naval Observatory in Washington, D.C., for a photo session where they would take pictures and then we could decide from all the poses which one he should paint. I was still living in D.C. at the time and getting ready to move out soon. When I came back from a run, they were setting up and so I went to be another set of eyes.

Dad kept teasing me and joking, "This will be at my funeral one day, Charlotte. Gotta make sure it's good."

I rolled my eyes and told him to stop. I didn't want to imagine that scenario, so I pushed the thought from my mind. The truth is that portrait probably will be there. I will smile to myself at the ceremony when I see it; I will remember his incessant teasing, just as he planned.

They set up everything with the props he had decided upon— his desk with a picture of his family, his open Bible, and his dad's old law books. He wore the tie my mom had designed when she was First Lady of Indiana and he was adamant his wedding ring be shown in the picture. When I arrived, he was trying out different poses leaning against the desk, sitting on it, and standing in front of it. I could tell he was feeling a little self-conscious. He wanted it to be authentic, to be true to himself and yet still convey a specific message to all those who would see it hanging in the State House throughout history.

I realized I needed to pull out the big guns for this task and ran upstairs to find the one person who can put him at ease no matter what situation.

Mom came down with me and waited quietly to the side. She walked around the camera and lighting equipment, stood behind the photographer, and smiled at Dad as the pictures were taken.

A few days later, we got the photos back and went through each one. We sent them around to members of our family and finally settled on the one that was painted: him sitting against the desk, his hands folded, ring finger visible, with a peaceful twinkle of joy in his eye. Looking back through all the photos, one thing was obvious: his expression in the one we chose was authentic. He was content.

As I scrolled through my phone to see the personal pictures I had taken during the session, I found the one with him sitting against the desk as he is in the portrait.

From the angle where I was standing, you can see the photographer snapping the picture that would be used to paint it.

Behind him, looking right at Dad with a soft smile is my mom.

The peaceful look in his eye is from looking at her.

And so it will be remembered forever. Whether at his funeral or in the Indiana State House with groups of schoolchildren walking through, his gaze will serve as a story, and hopefully, an example to keep one's sights on the things that matter most. It is easy to glance away, to lose sight of the important things in the stress of the day to day. Self-consciousness and anxiety can cloud our judgment if we don't actively remind ourselves to keep perspective. I hope to pass on these truths to my own children one day.

While it should make me sad to think about a time when Dad won't be here anymore, I know that for me, he always will be. His advice and character will live on and my faith tells me we won't be apart forever.

Spending so much time with my parents over the past year has made me wonder how I may be as a parent. I decided to take this opportunity to write a note to the family I hope to have one day. I know I will have children and I want to reach out to them now while I am still young and detached from parenthood.

A Letter to My Future Children:

Dear Kids,

When I was a little girl and adults asked me what I wanted to be when I grew up, I would tell them: "An author and a mom." Sometimes, I would add in that I wanted to have an orphanage and an alpaca farm, but it was mainly limited to those two things.

An author and your mom.

They would laugh at me sometimes, saying being a "mom" was not a job, but I never understood this. I still don't.

I want to let you know something.

It is a fact I will most likely regret admitting at a later date, when I want you to have utter faith in me, when I want you to see me in the best possible light.

Right now, I want you to know I am not without flaws.

There is no perfect person and I will make mistakes.

I hope you seek out the things that light a fire in your soul and I hope you find them at least once in your lives.

Know that each day will not be perfect or amazing. Know that there will be days you struggle and feel alone, but without those days, you won't rely on anyone else or on any faith you may come to have.

Keep true to what you know, to those around you, and rest assured I have done my best to add only positivity to your existence.

As my parents loved and taught me, so I will hope to do the same for you.

I hope their influence on my life reaches you.

Never let your dreams and inspirations be derailed by anyone who thinks little of you, for it is they who are blind and not you who are naive. Never let anyone tell you your dreams are "just a hobby." Go for those dreams. You have nothing to lose. And I'll be waiting for you when you fail, when you fall, when you need to be reminded that you can.

Take comfort in your willingness to dream and don't lose the wonder of a child when you strike out on your own.

I hope you know me to be one who has never lost it.

Love,
Mom

I want to be remembered for the life I lived and the people I met along the way. They are our legacy; their memory of us is the currency we leave behind. Keep seeking them out, keep reaching out to the ones you have already found, and remember that in your moments of doubt, a new face may be just around the corner, waiting to believe in you.

Chapter Twenty-Nine

Aim High

*And we know that in all things God works for the good of those
who love him, who have been called according to his purpose.*

—Romans 8:28

The life-changing twelve months from the start of our involvement in the 2016 election to the summer of 2017 held a lot for our family. They included travels all over the country and around the world. I met people who moved and inspired me and continue to do so in my career now. The year officially ended for me when I left home and moved out on my own.

I was scared. My life was going to be mine and mine only. I wasn't actively supporting another person in the way I had with Mom and Dad for the past year. I needed to be out there, answering questions for myself, having my own opinions, but I knew it was going to be a transition for me. Transitions, as I learned over the year, are the hardest part, but they are the times in which we grow the most.

As I got ready to move to Los Angeles (with no job, no

apartment, and no car), I thought of the obstacles I might encounter there. I decided it would be worth it and wrote the following in my journal before leaving home:

Opposition I can take, silence I cannot.

This accurately sums up my entire experience in the first year of this new journey for my family. And it can apply to anyone.

Let's not settle into the normal, easy routines of our lives.

Let's go out with gusto, ready to take on the world, encounter people who disagree with us and think differently.

Let's acknowledge that we are all different, that we have been raised in varying ways, and let's actively seek out those who make incorrect assumptions about us.

Let's remember that our lives are short, and imperfect, and beautiful, and strange.

Before I officially moved out, I confided in Dad more of my thoughts and dreams. I told him I was interested in studying more religious texts and learning about faith traditions so I could write with a more informed voice. I was considering applying to graduate school, but I knew I wanted to go to Los Angeles first before making that kind of decision. I wasn't sure where God was leading me at the time. I knew it was somewhere, and I knew where He called, I would go.

Dad agreed I should seek out all opportunities. I'll never forget what he said to me then. It was as if I had heard this piece of wisdom before, at another time, when we were unsure of the path ahead but knew if we followed it, we would end up in the right place, even though we didn't know where that would be.

His words to me could have been spoken to us at the onset of the 2016 election cycle. Perhaps, in a way, they were.

They were a whisper at the edge of the chasm that was our future.

They were a beckoning into the unknown where we had no guarantee things were going to end a certain way.

They were a divine promise then and they are now.

"Aim high," he said.

"The future beckons."

Afterword

It is now 2018 and I write this from Los Angeles. After living with my parents for a year after college, I moved to the West Coast to pursue a career in writing and entertainment. This is the path I always saw myself on. From a young age, I wanted to tell stories through film and books. I have changed my mind on many things in life, but never this.

I watched my parents' example, took their lead, and followed my dreams. They not only actively encourage their kids to chase after what they want in life, but they also live out this practice themselves. It is that which is the most inspiring.

Moving away was difficult. I missed my family and friends. I missed the snow and rain. I felt isolated at times, yet I never felt as if it was the wrong place to be. I knew God had called me into this field, into this chosen medium, and I will answer that call even when I don't know where it will lead.

I spent the first few months in Los Angeles working at a coffee shop and sleeping on an air mattress in a friend's spare room. I didn't have a car yet, so I took the bus whenever I needed to go somewhere. I started working in the mailroom at United Talent Agency a few months later and spent an incredible year learning the ins and outs of the entertainment industry from the experts. I made amazing friends whom I know I will remain close with throughout the years. We have that irreplaceable bond you find with people who forge a path on their own and bump into others doing the same thing along the way.

While I felt blessed to work in this field I love, I still felt a nagging sense in the back of my mind to look into graduate schools. On a whim, I applied and prayed I would end up wherever it was God was calling me. If that meant staying where I was, I was happy with that, too.

When this book is published, I will be starting at Harvard Divinity School studying for a master's in theological studies with a focus on religious themes in literature. It would appear God had been working in me and bringing this dream to life for some time, as can be seen through the writing of this book.

I don't wake up in the vice president's residence every day and I don't ride around in the armored vehicles my parents travel in. I get my news from the same sources everyone else does. I don't go to the White House as often or attend official events. I still talk to my parents every day, though, and we are as much a part of each other's lives as we were before.

Things are different, yet they are also the same.

Everything has changed, and nothing has changed.

May it always be so.

And may I always ask God where He is taking me.

And answer, wherever it is, "I will go."

Acknowledgments

I have a heart full of gratitude for everyone who has supported me in writing this book and putting down the stories of my treasured family to paper.

To Robert Wolgemuth and Austin Wilson, thank you for not only championing this project, but for your spiritual example as well. Virginia Bhashkar is an incredible editor and supportive advocate for the message I wanted to convey. Thank you to the entire Center Street and Hachette team for your steadfast work and dedication to this project.

I can never thank my parents enough for all they have given me. Thank you both for taking me along on the journey, for including us in every adventure and never failing to lead by example in all that you do. Mom, for your unrelenting listening and reading—not just of this book, but throughout my entire life. Dad, for the unhindered advice and unconditional love. Thank you for reminding me that I am a writer each time I start to forget. Audrey, Michael, and Sarah, for your willingness and eagerness and joy. Thank you for picking up the phone every time I call and for adding your perspective and memories to mine. I hope you see that you are on every page of this book and in every story I will ever tell.

Thank you, Nini, for being the unwavering matriarch of our family. Thank you for raising my dad to be the man he is and for offering your legacy to this project.

And thank you to my late grandfather, Poppa Pence, for the lessons of your life I am still learning. I can't wait to meet you one day.

To all the friends I have been blessed to do life with, thank you for coming along on the adventures. Amelia, Isaac, and my future goddaughter, your friendship is not something I deserve in the slightest and I thank God every day He led me to you in search for a random summer roommate in Los Angeles. Thank you for your love and care during this season of my life and the ones to come.

Charity, I thank you for being a shining light in all you do. Thanks for sticking with me—from first grade to now.

And last but never least: I cannot adequately express the gratitude I feel for my Savior, the One who calls us out onto the water, who guides our steps, and who never leaves us.

This, I hope, is a story of my family, yet I hope, even more so, it is a story of Him.

About the Author

CHARLOTTE PENCE is the *New York Times* bestselling author of *Marlon Bundo's A Day in the Life of the Vice President* (Regnery Publishing, 2018). Her work has also been published in *Glamour* magazine and featured in *US Weekly*, among other media outlets. A graduate of DePaul University with a BA in Digital Cinema Screenwriting and English, Charlotte contributed writing and production skills to the Emmy Award–winning documentary *Fleeced* (WFYI Productions). She recently accompanied her parents on the campaign trail across America, when her father, Vice President Mike Pence, ran for office alongside President Donald Trump. Charlotte lives in Cambridge, Massachusetts, where she attends Harvard Divinity School.